Appeals against the dismissal before the national courts have failed Jacob Guja. The courts decided that Guja's action was an abuse of his post and could not be regarded as a legitimate exercise of his freedom of speech.[29] The whistleblower brought an action before the European Court of Human Rights,[30] which ruled that his release violated the freedom of expression, in particular the freedom of information and communication guaranteed by the European Convention on Human Rights. The Court indicated that Jacob Guja acted in good faith and had no other effective means of drawing attention to the abuses. Moreover, the Court noted that the public interest in the discussed case outweighed the office's reputation loss caused by the disclosure of information. As a result of the ruling, the Moldavian State was obliged to pay the applicant €10,000 to compensate for material and non-material damage and more than €8,000 to reimburse costs and expenses. The whistleblower was subsequently reinstated, but after ten days the company fired him again. After using all possible national legal paths, once again, the case went to the European Court of Justice (ECJ). In his complaint, the man indicated that his reinstatement was an illusion and that the actions of the office continued previous sanctions imposed on him for his signaling activity. Some indicators of such situation appeared in the fact that his bosses assigned him no tasks and he did not even have access to the office. The ECJ held that – despite the alleged implementation of the previous ruling – the company never actually intended to reinstate Guja. Another dismissal was a further retaliatory measure for the whistle-blowing activity undertaken in 2003. Thus, the Court found that Article 10 of the European Convention for the Protection of Human Rights and Fundamental Freedoms had again been infringed.[31] This time, the Court obliged Moldavia to pay the applicant €10,000 for the damage suffered and €1,500 as reimbursement of costs and expenses.

29 Ploszka, "Ochrona" p. 15.

30 *Convention for the Protection of Human Rights and Fundamental Freedoms drew up by the Council of Europe and signed on November 4, 1950*; *Dziennik Ustaw* 61.284/1993.

31 *Convention for the Protection.*

In the literature, we can also find examples on the activity of Polish whistleblowers.[32] The publication *Wiem i powiem. Ochrona sygnalistów i dziennikarskich źródeł informacji* (I Know and Will Tell: The Protection of Whistleblowers and Journalistic Sources of Information) published by the Helsinki Foundation for Human Rights describes one of such examples.[33] The publication concerns a gynecologist who disclosed information on the fixing of a competition for the position of the gynecological ward head at one of the hospitals. After winning the competition, this person was to open a gynecological-oncological ward in the hospital, even though the facility was not adapted for this purpose. The whistleblower shared his information with the hospital authorities, the proper Medical Chamber, and during the session of the County Council. Despite the above, the person concerned won the competition.[34] However, the person was dismissed after a series of neglects that led to negative consequences for the health of patients. The whistleblower lost his job and was sued for defamation. Eventually, the court disputes ended favorably for him and, among other things, he was reinstated.

However, as evidenced by the results of the research[35] conducted in this field, it is difficult to consider this end of the case as representative of all the whistleblower cases in Poland. Further part of this study elaborates on that matter.

---

32 Kobylińska, Folta, *Sygnaliści*; R. Hryniewicz, K. Krak, *Sygnaliści w organizacji. Jak skutecznie wdrożyć system sygnalizowania nieprawidłowości?*, Must Read Media, Warszawa 2019; D. Głowacka, A. Ploszka, M. Sczaniecki, *Wiem i powiem. Ochrona sygnalistów i dziennikarskich źródeł informacji*, Helsińska Fundacja Praw Człowieka, Warszawa 2016; Ł. Kobroń, "Czy Polskę czeka era 'etycznych donosów?' Społeczno-prawne aspekty działania whistleblowera," *Zeszyty Naukowe Towarzystwa Doktorantów UJ. Nauki Społeczne*, 10/2015, Towarzystwo Doktorantów UJ, Kraków, pp. 81–92.

33 Głowacka, Ploszka, Sczaniecki, *Wiem*, p. 9.

34 Głowacka, Ploszka, Sczaniecki, *Wiem*, p. 9

35 A. Wojciechowska-Nowak, *Ochrona sygnalistów w doświadczeniu sędziów sądów pracy. Raport z badań*, Warszawa 2011.

Chapter I Whistleblower Protection in Selected Legislatures

1.1 Preliminary Remarks

Currently, there are many legal regulations in the world that are comprehensively or at least in part relate to the protection of whistleblowers. More and more countries have recently adopted special legislation to protect whistleblowers, example being Italy or France. We can observe a different approach to the issue in each country. Among other things, this is due to the historical experience of individual countries. Many European countries have experienced totalitarian regimes in the past, so it is not surprising that their citizens still feel uncomfortable with any form of disclosure.[36] These countries include Poland, whose legislation on the protection of whistleblowers is discussed later in this paper. Not without significance are also cultural factors that occur in individual countries. The literature indicates that all forms of "snitching" are negatively perceived, for instance, in Italy.[37]

The following analysis covers the legal regulations concerning the protection of whistleblowers in selected countries around the world, i.e. the USA, the United Kingdom, Romania, Slovenia, Ireland, Italy, and France. Moreover, the analysis presents the general assumptions of legal protection in this field adopted in several other countries.

---

36 C. Speckbacher, *Ochrona whistleblowerów w świetle prac GRECO*, 2009, p. 15, http://www.batory.org.pl/doc/Whistleblowing_mechanisms_REV2_for_Batory_POL.pdf, access: 20.12.2018.

37 Kutera, "Whisteblowing," pp. 136–137.

1.2 Whistleblower Protection in Selected Legislatures around the World

1.2.1 The United States of America

In the United States of America, there is an elaborate system of legal protection for people who report irregularities.[38] As the crime rate in accounting and corporate governance increased, the US government tended more to ensure the protection of whistleblowers. The issues of entities such as Enron and WorldCom generated interest in whistleblowers' activities among the public and, consequently, among politicians. However, the literature indicates that despite the benefits whistleblowers bring to society, their protection in the USA remains an "inconsistent legislative patchwork."[39] Let us note that there are many state and federal laws about reporting irregularities, which vary significantly.[40] However, laws in this field often interact with each other and overlap at the state and federal levels.[41] There is no single act that comprehensively covers all whistleblowers' activities throughout the country, in both public and private sectors regardless of the sector in which they operate. Among the most important acts that protect whistleblowers in the USA are The False Claims Act[42] (1863) and the

---

38 Kutera, "Whisteblowing," p. 130; M. Andrzejewski, "Whistleblowing, czyli demaskacja pracownicza w zarządzaniu zasobami ludzkimi," *Acta Universitatis Lodziensis. Folia Oeconomica* 288/2013, Wydawnictwo Uniwersytetu Łódzkiego, Łódź, p. 284; Kobroń, "Whistleblower," p. 296.

39 S. M. Boyne, "Financial Incentives and Truth-Telling: The Growth of Whistle-Blowing Legislation in the United States," in: *Whistleblowing: A Comparative Study, Ius Comparatum – Global Studies in Comparative Law 16*, eds. G. Thusing, G. Forst, Springer International Publishing, Cham, 2016, p. 280.

40 T. M. Dworkin, "US Whistleblowing: a Decade of Progress?" in: *A Global Approach to Public Interest Disclosure. What Can We Learn from Existing Whistleblowing Legislation and Research?*, ed. David B. Lewis, Edward Elgar Publishing Limited, Cheltenham, 2010, p. 36.

41 C. Henkel, "Whistleblower Rights and Protection under U.S. Law in the Private Sector," 2017, https://www.researchgate.net/publication/317449281_Whistleblower_Rights_and_Protection_Under_US_Law_in_the_Private_Sector, access: 12.12.2018.

42 *The False Claims Act*, 31 U.S.C. §§ 3729–3733, https://www.law.cornell.edu/uscode/text/31/3729, access: 12.12.2018.

Whisteblower Protection Act[43] (1989), which mainly refers to the public sector, along with the Sarbanes-Oxley Act[44] (2002) and the Dodd-Frank Act[45] (2010), which refer to the private sector.[46]

Besides strictly jurisdictional solutions, institutions also conduct activities[47] that result, for instance, in the establishment of the National Whistleblowing Center in 1988. It operates in the whole USA and seeks public support and legal aid for people reporting violations.[48] Moreover, there is the Office of Special Counsel,[49] which assists whistleblowers who work in state agencies.[50]

Due to the highly complex system of protection for whistleblowers in the USA, it would be impossible to analyze all the legislation in this area. For the purposes of this study, the following chapter contains only a general overview of the most important legal regulations in this field.

1.2.1.1 The False Claims Act

The starting point for the development of whistleblower protection in the USA is the False Claims Act, adopted by Congress on March 2, 1863. It is also known as the Lincoln Law. It is a federal law that encourages disclosure of irregularities.[51] This regulation is considered to have had recently the greatest impact on the protection of whistleblowers in the USA.[52] Originally, the law was a response to speculations of military contractors during the Civil War who tried to deceive the government, for example by sending

---

43 *Whistleblower Protection Act*, Pub. L. No. 101-12, 103 Stat. 16. https://www.usda.gov/oig/webdocs/whistle1989.pdf, access: 12.12.2018.

44 *Sarbanes-Oxley Act*, Pub. L. No. 107-204, 116 Stat. 745 (2002). https://www.govtrack.us/congress/bills/107/hr3763/text, access: 12.12.2018.

45 *Dodd-Frank Wall Street Reform and Consumer Protection Act*, Publ. L. No. 111-203, 124 Stat. 1376 (2010). https://www.govinfo.gov/content/pkg/BILLS-111hr4173enr/pdf/BILLS-111hr4173enr.pdf, access: 12.12.2018.

46 Kutera, "Whisteblowing," p. 130.

47 R. Dąbrowski, "Demaskacja jako narzędzie do walki z korupcją," *Kwartalnik Policyjny*, 3/2011, Centrum Szkolenia Policji, Legionowo, p. 42.

48 Information from: https://www.whistleblowers.org/, access: 20.06.2019.

49 Office's website: https://osc.gov/.

50 Dąbrowski, "Demaskacja," p. 42.

51 Dworkin, "US Whistleblowing," p. 43.

52 Boyne, "Financial Incentives," p. 285.

boxes of sawdust instead of weapons or repeatedly selling the same horse to the cavalry of the armed forces.[53] The Act authorized the citizens aware of such practices to take measures against such deceivers. The provisions of the Act underwent several modifications since 1863. Significant changes appeared in 1986 under the False Claims Reform Act of 1986.[54] Among others, the provisions aimed at facilitating cash recovery procedures for whistleblowers and, thus, encouraging more frequent reporting of fraudulent irregularities committed by government contractors.[55] It is worth noting that once the government recognized the success of the federal law, many states enacted similar regulations to combat local government fraud and reward whistleblowers.

The False Claims Act allows anyone aware of fraud against the government to file a lawsuit on their behalf. A claim brought under this Act by an individual whistleblower – also referred to as a relator[56] – is known as a *qui tam* claim. The concept of the *qui tam* dates back to the Middle Ages and comes from the Latin phrase "Qui tam pro domino rege quam pro seipse," which means "the one who sues in this case for both the king and himself."[57] Under this concept, government supports and protects citizens to

---

53 Ł. Kobroń-Gąsiorowska, "Whistleblower w prawie europejskim – ochrona whistleblowera czy informacji," *Roczniki Administracji i Prawa* 2/2018, Wyższa Szkoła Humanitas, Sosnowiec, p. 132; Becker's Hospital Review, "11 Things to Know About the False Claims Act," 2010, https://www.beckershospitalreview.com/news-analysis/eleven-things-to-know-about-the-false-claims-act.html, access: 19.08.2019.

54 31 U.S.C. §§ 3729-3733 (1986).

55 Dworkin, "US Whistleblowing," p. 43.

56 "The term "relator" is another word for whistleblowers. It originated in the False Claims Act whistleblower reward law signed by President Abraham Lincoln on March 2, 1863, during the Civil War. The term "whistleblower" was not in use in 1863. Consequently, in modern whistleblower reward laws, the term "relator" is often used by the Courts and parties to signify a whistleblower," https://www.whistleblowers.org/faq/false-claims-act-qui-tam/, access: 24.06.2019.

57 S. M. Kohn, *The Whistleblower`s Handbook: A Step-by-Step Guide to Doing What's Right and Protecting Yourself*, Lyons Press, Guilford, 2011; S. Mukherjee, *Protection of Whistleblowers in United States of America,* LAP LAMBERT Academic Publishing, Saarbrücken, 2013, p. 13.

help enforce the law the behalf of the state.[58] Consequently, the private individual is the one who initiates the proceedings. The government is legally obliged to examine the allegations made by the individual.[59] After considering all the circumstances, the Department of Justice decides whether to join the proceedings.[60] According to 31 U.S.C. § 3730 (c)(3), if the government decides not to proceed with the action, the initiator has the right to conduct it. However, if the Government decides to join the proceedings, it bears the main responsibility for prosecution and is not bound by the act of the person bringing the action.[61] Still, a private individual has the right to continue the proceedings as a party.[62] Before the expiration of the sixty-day period or any extension under the Act, the government should proceed with the action – in such case the action is taken by the government – or notify the court that it refuses to take over the action, in which case the person bringing the action has the right to take over the action.[63] The whistleblower acts anonymously for at least sixty days. This period may be extended by the court.[64] It follows from the above that the identity of the whistleblower is initially protected, yet it is disclosed at a later stage in the proceedings.

In § 3729(a), the False Claims Act indicates the liability for certain acts.[65] For instance, § 3729(a)(1)(A) & (B) makes liable anyone who knowingly made a false claim, or caused someone else to make a false claim, or knowingly made a false record or statement, in order to induce the government to pay a false claim. On the other hand, § 3729(a)(1)(G) is known as a section of reverse false claim.[66] In this case, liability arises when action is taken to avoid the obligation to pay money to the government.[67] Moreover,

58 Mukherjee, *Protection*, p. 13.
59 Boyne, "Financial Incentives," p. 287.
60 Boyne, "Financial Incentives," p. 287.
61 31 U.S.C. § 3730 (c)(1).
62 31 U.S.C. § 3730 (c)(1).
63 31 U.S.C. § 3730 (b)(4) (A) & (B).
64 31 U.S.C. § 3730 (b)(3).
65 The Department of Justice, *The False Claims Act: A Primer*, 2011. https://www.justice.gov/sites/default/files/civil/legacy/2011/04/22/C-FRAUDS_FCA_Primer.pdf, access: 14.06.2019.
66 *The False Claims Act.*
67 *The False Claims Act.*

the provisions of the Act prohibit employers from taking any discriminatory action. An employee who experiences such proceedings may bring a lawsuit before a court. A whistleblower seeking to sue his employer for retaliatory action against him must prove that he was engaged in activities protected by the False Claims Act and that the employer took retaliatory action due to knowledge of the *qui tam* action.[79] The identity of the whistleblower is disclosed by the court when the proceedings go beyond the investigation stage. However, we should remember that an employer may deduce the identity of a person disclosing information earlier, on the basis of its content.[80]

The civil action referred to the above may not be brought before court more than three years after the date of the retaliation's occurrence.[81] However, under § 3731(b), a whistleblower may not bring a fraud suit against the government after six years from the date of the violation or after three years from the date when the facts relevant to the right of action are known or should have been known to a US official entrusted with responsibility for action.[82] Under no circumstances may a claim be brought more than ten years after the date of infringement.[83]

1.2.1.2 The Whistleblower Protection Act

The US government passed the Whistleblower Protection Act in 1989.[84] This Act protects federal employees in the United States from retaliation resulting from disclosing information about fraudulent or illegal activities taking place within the federal administration. This Act, like the False Claims Act, is one of the most important US regulations for the protection of whistleblowers.

The law provides statutory protection for individuals who engage in whistleblowing, which means the disclosure of evidence of illegal or improper

---

79 Boyne, "Financial Incentives," p. 288.
80 Boyne, "Financial Incentives," p. 288.
81 31 U.S.C. § 3730 (h)(3).
82 31 U.S.C. § 3731 (b), Boyne, "Financial Incentives," p. 289.
83 31 U.S.C. § 3731 (b).
84 Pub. L. No. 101–12, 103 Stat. 16, later as: WPA.

government action.[85] Protection is extended to most current and former employees of the federal administration and listed state-owned enterprises, as well as to those, who apply for certain positions.[86] However, certain persons are excluded from the protection of this Act. These include, but are not limited to, employees of the Central Intelligence Agency (CIA), the National Security Agency (NSA), or individuals in positions legally excluded from the competitive federal service, because of their "confidential, policy-making, policy-shaping, or policy-supporting character."[87]

The Act provides protection from personnel action against certain persons or the lack of such action for the purpose of making a protected disclosure of information, i.e. informing about irregularities.[88] This includes a wide range of activities that have a negative impact on the employee. In accordance with U.S.C. 5. § 2302(a)(2)(A), prohibited human resources activities may include, but are not limited to promotion, transfer, reassignment, and any disciplinary action or decisions regarding compensation. People are protected from negative personnel actions, if they legally disclose information, about which they have a reasonable belief that they have evidence for:

- violation of any provision of law, rule, or regulation;
- gross mismanagement;[89]
- gross waste of funds;[90]

85 L. P. Whitaker, *The Whistleblower Protection Act: An Overview. CRS Report for Congress*, 2007, p. 1, https://fas.org/sgp/crs/natsec/RL33918.pdf, access: 24.07.2019.

86 M. Waszak, "Status osób ujawniających nieprawidłowości w miejscu pracy w Republice Słowackiej i jego ewolucja z perspektywy przepisów ustawy z dnia 16 października 2014 r.," *Zarządzanie Publiczne* 4(40)/2017, Wydawnictwo Uniwersytetu Jagiellońskiego, Kraków, p. 554.

87 5 U.S.C. § 2302(a)(2)(B); 5 U.S.C. § 2302(a)(2)(C), Boyne, "Financial Incentives," pp. 303–304.

88 5 U.S.C. § 2302(b)(8)(B), Whitaker, "The Whistleblower," p. 2.

89 Gross mismanagement is "a management action or inaction which creates a substantial risk of significant adverse impact upon the agency's ability to accomplish its mission." See Kavanagh v. M.S.P.B., 176 F. App'x 133, 135 (Fed. Cir. Apr. 10, 2006).

90 Gross waste of funds is a "more than debatable expenditure that is significantly out of proportion to the benefit reasonably expected to accrue to the government." See *Van Ee v. EPA*, 64 M.S.P.R. 693, 698 (1994).

- an abuse of authority;[91] or
- a serious and particular threat to public health or safety.[92]

However, the disclosure of information may not be explicitly prohibited by law[93] and may not be covered by secrecy for reasons of national defense or foreign affairs.[94] As indicated above, a person who discloses certain information must have a reasonable belief that the information is true. Whether or not the information ultimately proves to be true is irrelevant to the possibility of receiving protection, if the actions are taken in accordance with the provisions of the Act. The employee must only prove that the person in their place can reasonably believe – given the information available to them – that the information disclosed is indicative of one of the statutory types of misconduct.[95] If this condition is met, the burden of proof is shifted to the employer, who must prove with clear and convincing evidence that he would have taken the same action against the employee, even if the latter had not disclosed the information.[96] The Act also applies to the disclosure of irregularities to the Special Counsel,[97] the General Inspector of the agency or any other employee designated by the head of the agency to handle such disclosures.[98]

The whistleblower may seek legal protection under one of the following procedures: complaint due to an agency's negative action against

91 An abuse of authority is an "arbitrary or capricious exercise of power by a federal official or employee" that harms the rights of any person or that personally benefits the official/employee or their preferred associates. See Elkassir v. Gen. Servs. Admin., 257 F. App'x 326, 329 (Fed. Cir. Dec. 10, 2007).

92 5 U.S.C. § 2302(a)(8)(A).

93 To be "specifically prohibited by law" the information disclosed must be explicitly barred by a statute, as opposed to merely an agency rule or regulation. See Dep't of Homeland Sec. v. MacLean, 135 S. Ct. 913, 921 (2015).

94 5 U.S.C. § 2302(b)(8)(A).

95 *See Webb v. Dep't of the Interior*, 122 M.S.P.R. 248, 251 (2015); Lachance v. White, 174 F.3d 1378, 1380 (Fed. Cir. 1999).

96 5 U.S.C. 1214(b)(4)(B)(ii).

97 The Office of Special Counsel is an investigative and prosecutorial office that works to end government and political corruption and to protect government employees and whistleblowers; https://www.usa.gov/federal-agencies/office-of-special-counsel, access: 24.07.2019.

98 Boyne, "Financial Incentives," p. 304.

an employee to the Merit Systems Protection Board; action brought by the Office of Special Counsel; individually maintained right to lodge a complaint to the Merit Systems Protection Board; and, complaint brought by an employee under negotiated grievance procedures.[99]

Moreover, we should mention that in November 2012 Congress amended the Whistleblower Protection Act by adopting the Whistleblower Protection Enhancement Act.[100] The new version strengthened the protection of federal workers who disclose evidence of waste, fraud, or abuse.[101] The aim of WEPA was to close the gaps in the WPA that were exploited by managers and supervisors.[102] Among others, literature mentions the abolition of the Federal Circuit Court monopoly on appeals,[103] the extension of protection to Transportation Safety Administration staff and the obligation for the Inspectors General Offices to appoint an Ombudsman for the protection of whistleblowers in order to educate staff in the field of whistleblower protection.[104] The role of the Whistleblower Ombudsman is to educate agency staff about prohibited retaliation for disclosures, and about their rights and remedies in the event of retaliation for reporting irregularities.[105] Moreover, the Office of Special Counsel has been granted the right to act as a "friend of the court" *amicus curiae* at the appeal stage, if the whistleblower lost the administrative hearing stage.[106]

---

99 Whitaker, "The Whistleblower."

100 Pub. L. Nr 112–199, 126 Stat. 1465 (2012). https://www.govinfo.gov/content/pkg/PLAW-112publ199/pdf/PLAW-112publ199.pdf, access: 24.07.2019. Later referred to as: WEPA.

101 https://www.justice.gov/pardon/whistleblower-protection-enhancement-act, access: 12.07.2019.

102 Boyne, "Financial Incentives," p. 305.

103 Information from: https://www.whistleblower.org/uncategorized/whistleblower-protection-enhancement-act-wpea/, access: 15.07.2019.

104 Boyne, "Financial Incentives," p. 305.

105 Information from: U.S. Consumer Product Safety Commission, "Whistleblower Protections," https://www.cpsc.gov/About-CPSC/Inspector-General/Whistleblower-Protection-Act-WPA, access: 15.07.2019.

106 Boyne, "Financial Incentives," p. 305.

and Exchange Commission (SEC).[120] Pursuant to section 806 of the SOX, the protection applies to employees who have a reasonable suspicion that they report activities that violate:

- any federal criminal law provisions prohibiting postal fraud, bank transfer or bank fraud;
- any rules or regulations of the Securities and Exchange Commission (SEC); or
- any federal laws related to shareholder fraud.[121]

A whistleblower must be guided in their actions by a reasonable belief that their employer has committed fraud. In order to satisfy the requirement to act with a reasonable belief, a whistleblower must genuinely believe that the conduct he has noticed constitutes an infringement, and that a reasonable person in their position and with the same education would consider that the conduct in question constitutes an infringement. The case law has pointed out in this context that, "[a] belief that an activity was illegal may be reasonable even when subsequent investigation proves a complainant was entirely wrong. The accuracy or falsity of the allegations is immaterial; the plain language of the regulations only requires an objectively reasonable belief that shareholders were being defrauded to trigger the Act's protections."[122] However, whistleblower's mere raising of general doubts as to the regularity of a particular transaction without indicating any specific reasons for concern is insufficient.[123] This implies a requirement that the information disclosed must meet a certain minimum degree of concreteness.

For instance, a whistleblower may provide evidence of fraud to a supervisor, another employee, "who has the authority to investigate, discover, or terminate misconduct," federal regulatory or law enforcement authority,

120 In 2010, protection was extended to employees of a subsidiary, if its finances are included in the parent company's financial statement.

121 18 U.S.C. § 1514A (2002); Boyne, "Financial Incentives," p. 290.

122 Halloum v. Intel Corp., 2003-SOX-7, (ALJ March 4, 2004); qtd. after G. R. Watchman, *Sarbanes-Oxley Whistleblowers: Avoiding the Nightmare Scenario*, 2008, p. 10, http://media01.commpartners.com/acc_webcast_docs/SOX_paper.pdf, access: 12.05.2019.

123 Lerbs v. Buca Di Beppo, 2004-SOX-8 (ALJ June 15, 2004).

a member of Congress, or any congressional committee.[124] As can be seen from the above, the Act gives whistleblowers a relatively large amount of freedom to choose the addressee of the disclosure.

SOX prohibits any retaliation against whistleblowers resulting from their disclosure activities and it grants them special protection.[125] Anyone who knowingly takes any action harmful to a whistleblower with intent to retaliate risks increased civil and criminal liability.[126] The Act broadly covers retaliatory measures, which include[127] dismissal, demotion, suspension, threatening, harassment, or any other form of discrimination against an employee connected with employment conditions due to the reporting of misconduct under the Act. The case law indicates that one of the actions not prohibited by the Act is the negative periodic assessment of an employee, if it does not contribute to the deterioration of the employee's employment conditions.[128] The provisions of the Act that prohibit retaliation against whistleblowers cover both legal persons and natural persons associated with the employer.[129] The prohibition applies to companies, but also to their officers, other employees, contractors, subcontractors, and agents of such companies.[130]

The Act provides that a whistleblower who suffered negative consequences for their actions may file a written complaint to the Secretary of Labor not later than ninety days later. Under the terms of the Dodd-Frank Act from 2010, this period was extended to 180 days. The period commences on the date on which retaliation happens or on the date on which the employee becomes aware of the retaliation.[131] If the Secretary of Labor did not make a final decision within 180 days of the date of the complaint and "there

124 18 U.S.C. § 1514A (2002).

125 SOX, Section 806 Protection for Employees of Publicly Traded Companies Who Provide Evidence of Fraud, Section 1107 Retaliation Against Informants.

126 18 U.S.C. § 1513 (e). The law provides for high fines and prison sentences of up to ten years., M. Kutera, "Whisteblowing," p. 131.

127 18 U.S.C. § 1514A (a).

128 Dolan v. EMC Corp., 2004-SOX-1 (ALJ March 24, 2004).

129 W. Rogowski, "Whistleblowing: bohaterstwo, zdrada czy interes?," *Przegląd Corporate Governance* 1/2007, Fundacja Polski Instytut Dyrektorów, p. 34.

130 18 U.S.C. § 1514A (a).

131 18 U.S.C. § 1514A (b)(2)(d).

is no showing that such delay is due to the bad faith of the claimant," the employee may file a lawsuit with the appropriate federal court.[132] The court shall then deal with the case irrespective of the value of the matter at issue.[133] The literature stresses that making it possible for whistleblowers to exercise their rights in this way was an innovative solution.[134]

If the Secretary makes a decision in favor of an employee, the latter shall be entitled to all necessary remedies to protect them.[135] The remedies include:

a) reinstatement to work with the same length of service as the employee would have had he not been retaliated against;
b) payment of outstanding remuneration with interest; and
c) compensation for any damage suffered as a result of discrimination, including legal costs, fees of experts, and lawyer fees.[136]

However, practice shows that proceedings rarely end at this point, as parties to a dispute have a wide range of appeal possibilities against a decision of the Secretary.[137]

1.2.1.4 The Dodd-Frank Wall Street Reform and Consumer Protection Act

The Dodd-Frank Wall Street Reform and Consumer Protection Act[138] signed by President Barack Obama on July 21, 2010, was a response to the 2008 financial crisis.[139] It aimed to transform the US regulatory system in a number of areas, including, but not limited to, consumer protection, trade restrictions, credit ratings, financial product regulation, corporate

132 18 U.S.C. § 1514A (b)(1)(b).
133 Wojciechowska-Nowak, *Jak zdemaskować szwindel?*, p. 36.
134 Boyne, "Financial Incentives," p. 36.
135 18 U.S.C. § 1514A(c)(1).
136 18 U.S.C. § 1514A(c)(2).
137 For more, see Boyne, "Financial Incentives," p. 292.
138 Dodd-Frank Wall Street Reform and Consumer Protection Act, Pub. L. No. 111-203, 124 Stat. 1376 (2010).
139 The name comes from the names of Congressman Barney Frank and Senator Christopher J. Dodd.

governance, disclosure, and transparency.[140] The adoption of the law was also a further significant step towards enhancing the protection of whistleblowers in the United States. Although the Act primarily regulated functioning of financial markets and protection of consumer interests, it also contained protection measures and a number of incentives for whistleblowers.[141] Pursuant to section 922, a new section 21F was added to the Securities Trading Act of 1934. The Act gave whistleblowers increased protection against employer retaliation, guaranteed confidentiality, and provided the opportunity to receive a financial award.[142]

Section 15 U.S.C. § 78u-6(a)(6) of the Dodd-Frank Act defines the term "whistleblower" as one or more individuals acting jointly, who provide information about a violation of securities laws to the Commission [SEC][143] in a way determined by rule or regulation of the Commission.[144] Furthermore, according to the regulations issued by the SEC after the adoption of this law, a whistleblower must have a "reasonable belief" that the aforementioned regulations have been infringed.[145] Only natural persons may report infringements.

The Dodd-Frank Act prohibits retaliatory measures against whistleblowers, who disclose information of violations in accordance with procedures. Whistleblowers who experience such retaliation have the right to be reinstated with the length of service they would have enjoyed had they not disclosed the information, double the amount of outstanding wages with interest, along with compensation for legal fees, litigation costs,

---

140 Information from the website: U.S. Securities and Exchange Commission, "The Laws That Govern the Securities Industry," https://www.sec.gov/answers/about-lawsshtml.html#sox2002, access: 12.07.2019.

141 P. Chmiel, "Sygnalizowanie nieprawidłowości (whistleblowing)," *Przegląd Antykorupcyjny* 7/2016, Wydawnictwo Centrum Szkolenia Policji w Legionowie, Warszawa, p. 41.

142 OECD (2016), *Committing,* p. 109; Ł. Cichy, *Whistleblowing w bankach*, Komisja Nadzoru Finansowego, Warszawa 2017, p. 10, Kutera, "Whisteblowing," p. 132.

143 Securities and Exchange Commission, further referred to as: SEC.

144 National Whistleblower Center, "SEC Whistleblower/Dodd-Frank Act Reward Law," https://www.whistleblowers.org/faq/sec-whistleblower-dodd-frank-act/, access: 15.08.2019.

145 17 C.F.R § 240.21 F-2(b)(l), Boyne, "Financial Incentives," p. 302.

and court fees.[146] The protection against retaliation covers whistleblowers regardless of whether they have reported violations internally within the company or directly to the SEC.[147]

A particularly effective way of encouraging whistleblowers to act was to create the possibility of receiving financial incentive for the actions.[148] Providing important and previously unknown information to SEC by an authorized whistleblower – which leads to the imposition of sanctions on the entity infringing the law in a specified manner – entitles the person who reports the irregularities to receive a reward of 10–30 % of the funds, which the entity will be forced to pay for its infringements.[149] Whistleblowers may receive a financial award if their information leads to effective securities law enforcement actions.[150] The Act authorized the Commission to grant financial awards to eligible individuals if the sanctions imposed exceed one million dollars.[151] A high level of potential reward that a whistleblower may receive is intended to secure the existence of such a person in the event of loss of job, breakdown of professional career or even the need to change the place of residence.[152] SEC may exercise its freedom in determining the appropriate percentage of the award and take into account a number of factors in relation to the specific facts and circumstances of each reported case. Factors that may increase the amount of the prize include:

- the importance of provided information;
- the assistance given by the whistleblower;
- the interest of law enforcement authorities; and
- the participation in internal compliance systems.[153]

---

146 OECD (2016), *Committing*, p. 110.

147 The Securities and Exchange Commission, Interpretation of the SEC`s Whistleblower Rules under Section 21F of the Securities Exchange Act of 1934, www.sec.gov/rules/interp/2015/34-75592.pdf, access: 17.08.2019, OECD (2016), *Committing*, p. 110.

148 Kutera, "Whisteblowing," p. 132.

149 OECD (2016), *Committing*, p. 110.

150 Boyne, "Financial Incentives," p. 301.

151 Dodd-Frank Act §§ 748, 922.

152 Chmiel, "Sygnalizowanie," p. 42.

153 Art. 21F-6(a) Securities Exchange Act of 1934, U.S. Securities and Exchange Commission, "Regulation 21F," https://www.sec.gov/about/offices/owb/reg-21f.pdf, access: 12.07.2019.

On the other hand, factors that may reduce the amount of a whistleblower's award are:

- their guilt;
- unjustified delay in reporting a violation;
- violation of internal compliance and reporting systems by the whistleblower.[154]

The order of the above criteria does not determine their validity. It should be noted that some whistleblowers are excluded from the possibility to receive an award.[155] Among others, these are:[156]

- certain US law enforcement officers;
- employees of foreign governments;
- people convicted in criminal actions related to the information provided to the SEC; and
- certain auditors, including those who would violate Sections 10A of the Exchange Act by reporting information to the commission in order to obtain a whistleblower reward.

Moreover, the Dodd-Frank Act provides a possibility of anonymous transmission of information to the SEC by a counsel.[157] However, prior to payment of the award, the whistleblower discloses their identity and other information that SEC may request, either directly or by their counsel.[158]

It should be noted that the Dodd-Frank Act has strengthened and extended the regulation of whistleblowers' activities under the Sarbanes-Oxley Act. This includes, for example, the protection of employees of a subsidiary under the SOX rules if its finances are included in the financial statements of the parent company. Moreover, a whistleblower who accuses a company of retaliatory action resulting from a SOX-protected report receives the opportunity to sue directly in a federal court without exhausting

154 Art. 21F-6(b) Securities Exchange Act of 1934, U.S. Securities and Exchange Commission, "Regulation 21F," https://www.sec.gov/about/offices/owb/reg-21f.pdf. The order of the indicated criteria does not determine their importance.
155 Art. 21F-8 Securities Exchange Act of 1934.
156 OECD (2016), *Committing*, p. 110.
157 OECD (2016), *Committing*, p. 110.
158 15 U.S.C. § 78u-6(d)(2).

administrative resources.[159] Another change is the extension of the period from ninety to 180 days after the detection of an infringement during which whistleblowers have the right to lodge a claim.

Moreover, the Dodd-Frank Act strengthened the provisions of the False Claims Act, among other things, by amending section 3730(h) by ensuring the protection of whistleblower's colleagues.[160]

1.2.2 The United Kingdom

The protection of people who disclose perceived wrongdoings in the United Kingdom is universally considered to be one of the most developed in Europe.[161] The regulations in this respect were included above all in three legal acts:[162] the Public Interest Disclosure Act of 1998,[163] the Employment Rights Act of 1996,[164] and the Enterprise and Regulatory Reform Act of 2013.[165] The United Kingdom was the first European state which introduced a regulation strictly related to the protection of whistleblowers,[166] that is

159 Boyne, "Financial Incentives," p. 302.

160 31 U.S.C. § 3730 (h), Boyne, "Financial Incentives," p. 301.

161 M. Waszak, "Związki zawodowe i organizacje pracodawców a ustawy o ochronie sygnalistów. Przykłady europejskie," in: *Sygnaliści w Polsce okiem pracodawców i związków zawodowych*, eds. G. Makowski, M. Waszak, Fundacja im. Stefana Batorego, Warszawa 2016, p. 40; J. J. Wojciechowicz, "Sytuacja sygnalistów w kontekście międzynarodowym," in: *Systemy zgłaszania nieprawidłowości. Założenia do ustawy o ochronie sygnalistów*, p. 12, https://ungc.org.pl/wp-content/uploads/2018/09/Za%C5%82o%C5%BCenia-do-ustawy-o-oschronie-sygnalist%C3%B3w.pdf, access: 16.08.2019.

162 Kutera, "Whisteblowing," p. 137.

163 Online access to the text of the Act: https://www.legislation.gov.uk/ukpga/1998/23/introduction. Later referred to as: PIDA.

164 Online access to the text of the Act: http://www.legislation.gov.uk/ukpga/1996/18/contents. Later referred to as: the Act of 1996.

165 Online access to the text of the Act: http://www.legislation.gov.uk/ukpga/2013/24/contents.

166 L. Rossi, J. McGuinn, M. Fernandes, *Estimating the Economic Benefits of Whistleblower Protection in Public Procurement. Final Report – Study*, 2017, p. 87, https://publications.europa.eu/en/publication-detail/-/publication/8d5955bd-9378-11e7-b92d-01aa75ed71a1/language-en, access: 14.07.2019.

the Public Interest Disclosure Act (PIDA).[167] Its objective was to protect public interest by quickly discovering and stopping wrongdoings in private enterprises or public institutions; similarly to American regulations.[168] The PIDA fits into the British legislation on employment. Pursuant to its provisions, the Employment Rights Act of 1996 was amended.[169] Moreover, it was significantly amended on June 25, 2013, as the result of the Enterprise and Regulatory Reform Act. Among the most important introduced changes at that time was the introduction of "a public interest test," that is the obligation of an employee to demonstrate their belief that they disclose information in public interest, and the abolition of the criterion of good faith that was previously in force, whose application was limited by the above amendment only to the purposes of determining the amount of compensation for whistleblowers.[170]

The definition of an employee who is protected under the Public Interest Disclosures Act is broader than the definition in the Act of 1996 and covers people employed in all sectors, except for self-employed, volunteers, and employees of armed forces and intelligence service.[171] Below, within the scope of the term "an employee" or "a whistleblower," this text always includes all protected groups, regardless of the legal basis of their employment.

In the discussed Act, there are terms of protected disclosure and qualifying disclosure. Protected disclosure means a qualifying disclosure (in accordance with the definition included in Article 43B) made by an employee in accordance with the requirements specified in Articles 43C–43H of the Act. These requirements concern the making of disclosure to particular entities

---

167 The Act entered into force on July 2, 1999, in the United Kingdom and then a similar form of protection was implemented in the Northern Ireland on October 31, 1999.

168 A. Wojciechowska-Nowak, *Jak zdemaskować szwindel? Czyli krótki przewodnik po whistle-blowingu*, Fundacja im. Stefana Batorego, Warszawa 2008, p. 38; R. Dąbrowski, "Demaskacja jako narzędzie do walki z korupcją," *Kwartalnik Policyjny* 3/2011, Centrum Szkolenia Policji, Legionowo, p. 42.

169 Blueprint for Free Speech, "United Kingdom – Whistleblowing Protection," 2014, https://blueprintforfreespeech.net/document/united-kingdom, access: 13.07.2019.

170 Waszak, "Związki zawodowe", p. 43.

171 Waszak, "Związki zawodowe", p. 41.

and the fulfilment of certain conditions. The provisions of the Act provide a number of people to whom wrongdoings may be disclosed, depending on the circumstances.

In accordance with Article 43B of the Act of 1996, "qualifying disclosure" means the disclosure of information which – following the reasonable belief of an employee who makes the disclosure in public interest – will prove one or several of the following circumstances:

1. an offence was committed, is committed, or presumably will be committed;
2. a person failed, fails, or presumably will fail to comply with any legal obligation that he is subject to;
3. there occurred, occurs, or may occur a miscarriage of justice;
4. the health or security of any person was, is, or may be at risk;
5. the environment was, is, or may be damaged; or
6. information that any issue which falls within the scope of any of the above points was, is, or may be deliberately concealed.

In accordance with the above, the disclosed information may turn out to not be true. In order to grant protection to whistleblowers, only a reasonable belief of the wrongdoing occurrence is required. Moreover, we should emphasize that an offence may take place outside of the United Kingdom. It does not matter if other than British law is applied in a case of a wrongdoing.[172]

The protection will not apply if, while disclosing, a whistleblower commits an offence in the form of breaking the Official Secrets Act of 1989[173] or the regulations in force in the public office.[174]

Moreover, the disclosure of information, in which the claim for keeping the legal professional privilege may be sustained in legal proceedings, does not constitute qualifying disclosure, if it is made by a person who disclosed such information as a result of receiving legal advice.[175] Whistleblower will

---

172 Article 43B Paragraph 2 of the Employment Rights Act.

173 Online access to the text of the Act: https://www.legislation.gov.uk/ukpga/1989/6/contents.

174 Waszak, "Związki zawodowe", p. 40.

175 Article 43B Paragraph 4 of the Employment Rights Act.

not be protected, if they are convicted of committing such an offence or if – on the basis of presented evidence – a court is convinced that the whistleblower committed such an offence.

We should also indicate that the PIDA recognizes as qualifying disclosure only confidential disclosure that is not anonymous, which requires greater trust towards addressees.[176] It seems that this measure is aimed at discouraging the anonymous disclosure of wrongdoings, because it may make it impossible to determine significant issues in the scope of the disclosed wrongdoings. Moreover, the confidentiality of the disclosure does not have an absolute character, which enables holding those people liable who disclose information, should their actions turn out to be e.g. malicious.

The PIDA offers the following modes of disclosing information with increasing thresholds of protection:[177]

1) internal disclosure of information to employers;
2) disclosure of information to an appointed external body (of regulatory character) or a member of Parliament; and
3) a broader disclosure of information e.g. to the police, the media, or a non-governmental organization.[178]

Whistleblowers are encouraged to first undertake internal actions by means of certain restrictions for disclosing wrongdoings outside of workplace.[179] Internal disclosure consists of a whistleblower passing information about perceived wrongdoings on the forum of the organization.[180] Such a disclosure will be protected, should the whistleblower truly believe it will prove that a malpractice occurred, occurs, or presumably will occur. Pursuant to Article 43C Paragraph 1a of the Act of 1996, qualifying disclosure occurs, should an employee disclose information to his employer. However, if the employee has justified reasons to think that the wrongdoings concern solely or above all actions of a different person than his employer, or matters

176 Cichy, *Whistleblowing w bankach*, p. 10.
177 OECD (2016), *Committing to Effective Whistleblower Protection*, OECD Publishing, Paris, p. 105.
178 Waszak, "Związki zawodowe", p. 40.
179 Wojciechowicz, "Sytuacja sygnalistów," p. 12.
180 Dąbrowski, "Demaskacja," p. 38.

that a different person than his employer is legally responsible for, then he discloses information to the relevant person.[181] On the other hand, Article 43C Paragraph 2 constitutes that the employee who – on the basis of a procedure authorized by the employer – makes qualifying disclosure to other person than the employer, must be treated like a person who makes qualifying disclosure to the employer. The above provisions establish that – as a result of informing the management of the employer about the perceived wrongdoings – the management will take steps to clarify the presented information and eliminate potential threats. The objective is to discourage actions undertaken to harm the institution and enable their early detection.[182]

The implementation of special internal procedures of disclosure examination by employers should be recognized as a good practice. Even though the PIDA does not impose an obligation to establish such procedures, encouraging employees to report wrongdoings within the organization is in the interest of the employers. A lack of such a procedure may make whistleblowers disclose the issue outside of their workplace.[183]

Moreover, employees of state bodies will have protection, should they directly inform about their concerns a superior ministry and not their employer. It seems that the objective of the implementation of such regulations is to increase the certainty in the examination of the issue and the elimination of potential wrongdoings. If a whistleblower encounters negative consequences in result of disclosing information in such a way, their claim may be directed against the employer, not against the minister to whom he disclosed information.[184]

On the other hand, Article 43D of the Act of 1996 constitutes that qualifying disclosure also occurs if it is made during the reception of legal advice. The regulations enable employees to receive legal advice on wrongdoings perceived by them and to receive legal protection from potential negative consequences. When an employee authorizes their lawyer to further

---

181 Article 43C Paragraph 1b of the Employment Rights Act.

182 Wojciechowska-Nowak, *Jak zdemaskować szwindel?*, p. 44.

183 Waszak, "Związki zawodowe", p. 41.

184 Protect, "A guide to PIDA," https://www.whistleblowing.org.uk/a-guide-to-pida/, access: 13.07.2019.

disclosure of information, e.g. to the media or the employer himself, the actions of the lawyer are considered as undertaken on behalf and for the benefit of the employee.[185]

The provisions impose more rigorous conditions on employees who disclose information outside of the organization.[186] In such a case, the protection is granted to a whistleblower, if they disclose to a prescribed person, indicated in a special register,[187] and truly believe that a relevant offence falls within the scope of matters to which such a person was appointed, and that the disclosed information and all included allegations are substantially true. What follows from the above is that whistleblowers may turn to a prescribed person with an issue within the scope of its competences. In this regard, certain institutions should be indicated, such as those that act in areas of finances, health services, environmental protection, insurance, or consumer rights, including local government.[188] To obtain legal protection, whistleblowers must have reasonable belief that information and all included allegations are substantially true and relevant for the regulatory body.[189] Let us indicate that contacting bodies not in the register is qualified as disclosure to the wide audience, which results in a necessity to fulfil more rigorous conditions.[190]

However, in a case of disclosure to the wide audience, whistleblowers omit not only their employer but also proper supervisory bodies, and they present observed wrongdoings to e.g. the police or the media in order to popularize the issue and gain special attention.[191] The whistleblower when deciding on this path of disclosure – in order to receive protection – must demonstrate the important reasons that prevented him from informing in

---

185 Wojciechowska-Nowak, *Jak zdemaskować szwindel?*, p. 46.
186 Waszak, "Związki zawodowe", p. 40.
187 Department for Business, Energy & Industrial Strategy, *Blowing the Whistle to a Prescribed Person. List of Prescribed Person and Bodies*, 2018, https://www.gov.uk/government/publications/blowing-the-whistle-list-of-prescribed-people-and-bodies--2/whistleblowing-list-of-prescribed-people-and-bodies, access: 13.07.2019.
188 Waszak, "Związki zawodowe", p. 40.
189 OECD (2016), *Committing to*, p. 105.
190 Wojciechowska-Nowak, *Jak zdemaskować szwindel?*, p. 44.
191 Dąbrowski, "Demaskacja," p. 38.

the first place his employer or the supervisory body.[192] In such a case, the protection is granted to whistleblowers, if:

1) they have reasonable belief that the disclosed information and all included allegations are substantially true;
2) the disclosure is not for personal gain; and
3) all circumstances suggest that it is reasonable to disclose information, and one of the following conditions is met:

   (a) at the moment of disclosure, the employee has reasonable grounds to think that they will suffer harm from the employer if the information is disclosed to this employer or a prescribed person;
   (b) should nobody be provided for the objective of Article 43F – disclosure to a prescribed person – concerning a given offence, the employee has justified reasons to think that proofs connected to the given offence will presumably be concealed or destroyed if disclosed to the employer; or
   (c) the employee previously disclosed the same information to the employer or to the prescribed person.

When determining whether – in all circumstances of the issue – it was reasonable to disclose information, courts consider, among other things, the identity of the person to whom the information was disclosed, the significance of the offence, and whether it still occurs or presumably will occur in the future.[193] Noteworthy, the required degree of the offence's significance will be lower when the disclosure is made to the police than if the same information is disclosed to the media.[194]

The provisions of the Act of 1996 also guarantee protection in the case of disclosing information that does not meet the above conditions, if it concerns exceptionally serious offenses. In accordance with Article 43H of the Act, the qualifying disclosure will take place if the employee:

- has justified reasons to think that disclosed information and all included allegations are substantially true;

192 Wojciechowska-Nowak, *Jak zdemaskować szwindel?*, p. 44.
193 Article 43G Paragraph 3 of the Employment Rights Act.
194 Protect, "A guide to PIDA," https://www.whistleblowing.org.uk/a-guide-to-pida/, access: 13.07.2019.

- does not disclose information for personal gain;
- discloses an offence of exceptionally serious character and it is reasonable to disclose information in all circumstances of the issue.

On the other hand, Paragraph 2 of the Article constitutes that – during the examination whether the disclosure of information in all circumstances of the issue is reasonable –the identity of the person to whom the information is disclosed is specifically considered; e.g. the police or the press. The provisions do not contain any particular guidelines on the basis of which a given offence may be recognized as "particularly serious." This issue is decided individually for every case.[195]

In accordance with the British legislation, a dismissal of a person disclosing cases of violations will be recognized as unfair if its only or main reason is the fact that a whistleblower made a protected disclosure. Moreover, employees are also protected from suffering any other detriment related to the whistleblowing activity, e.g. making threats or limiting promotion opportunities. People who make protected disclosures in accordance with the provisions of the PIDA and were dismissed or suffered other detriment due to their whistleblowing activity may file a complaint to employment tribunals, which deal with the issues of whistleblowers in the United Kingdom. In their jurisprudence, employment tribunals are limited to deciding on the occurrence of the detriment of whistleblowers and on the amount of due compensation; i.e. they do not decide on the wrongdoings identified by employees.[196]

In accordance with Article 47B introduced by the PIDA to the Act of 1996, an employee has the right for his situation not to deteriorate due to any action or any deliberate negligence on the part of the employer,

195 Protect, "Raising exceptionally serious concerns. 43H of the Public Interest Disclosure Act 1998," https://protect-advice.org.uk/raising-exceptionally-serious-concerns-43h-of-the-public-interest-disclosure-act-1998, access: 25.06.2019.

196 Transparency International, *Providing an Alternative to Silence: Towards Greater Protection and Support for Whistleblowers in the EU. Country Report: United Kingdom*, Public Concern at Work, 2013, p. 2, https://www.asktheeu.org/en/request/994/response/5851/attach/4/Country%20report%20the%20UK.pdf, access: 20.05.2019.

undertaken on the basis of the protected disclosure made by the employee. Noteworthy, the employer will be also held responsible in a case when the employee, after informing about wrongdoings, is exposed to detriment colleagues, e.g. intimidation or harassment. Such an activity is treated as also made by the employer.[197] It does not matter if it happened with the knowledge or permission of the employer.[198] The employer may defend himself by indicating that he undertook all reasonable steps to avoid detriment due to the abovementioned actions.[199]

If the employment tribunal recognizes the complaint of an employee as valid, it may grant him compensation from the employer.[200] Its amount is established based on what is just and right in all circumstances of the issue, taking into consideration the violation that is the subject of the complaint and also every detriment suffered by the whistleblower due to the deterioration of his situation.[201] Compensation should cover in particular reasonable costs bore by the whistleblower or lost profits – e.g. the remuneration for the unemployment period – which he could expect if he did not lose the job or did not experience other victimized actions of the employer.[202] Noteworthy, recognized compensation is not subject to the statutory limit that is applied in standard claims of unjustified dismissal.[203] However, we should remember that the employment tribunal has the right to reduce all compensations even by 25 %, if it deems that the protected disclosure of information was not made in good faith.[204] In the case of litigation, the employer must provide proof. He must explain in front of the tribunal the reasons for which he undertook negative activities towards the whistleblower and prove that they were not the consequence of the disclosure of information.[205]

---

197 Article 47B Paragraph 1B of the Employment Rights Act.
198 Article 47B Paragraph 1C of the Employment Rights Act.
199 Article 47B Paragraph 1D of the Employment Rights Act.
200 Article 49 Paragraph 1 of the Employment Rights Act.
201 Article 49 Paragraph 2 of the Employment Rights Act.
202 Wojciechowska-Nowak, *Jak zdemaskować szwindel?*, pp. 47–48.
203 Save Us Now, "UK Rights and remedies for whistleblowers," 2019, https://www.saveusnow.org.uk/uk-rights-and-remedies-for-whistleblowers/, access: 12.07.2019.
204 OECD (2016), *Committing to*, p. 106.
205 Wojciechowska-Nowak, *Jak zdemaskować szwindel?*, p. 49.

1.2.3 Romania

Another European country that has regulations on whistleblower protection is Romania. The relevant act is the Law No. 571/2004 regarding the protection of the staff of the public authorities, public institutions, and other units that notifies breaches of the law.[206] This regulation is the result of actions undertaken to fight corruption in public administration. The provisions of the Law No. 571/2004 enable one the disclosure of a broad scope of wrongdoings and provide protection from retaliation. However, this protection is limited to individuals of the public sector.[207] Although, private entities have the possibility of implementing solutions from the public sector in their internal regulations.[208]

Article 3 of the Law No. 571/2004 includes a definition of disclosure in public interest, which should be recognized as disclosing in good faith the case of unlawful activity, violation of ethical professional standards or the principles of good administration, productivity, effectivity, economy, and transparency. Not all disclosed information may be protected.[209] Pursuant to Article 5 of the Law No. 571/2004, the disclosed wrongdoings may concern:

a) actions of corruptive character or actions connected to such or to ones directly related to them, frauds, breaches of responsibilities, or professional responsibilities related to the breach;
b) unlawful actions against the financial interest of the European Community;
c) practices or treatment which privileges or discriminates individuals listed in Article 2 of the Law;
d) breaking of provisions concerning *incompatibilitas* and the conflict of interest;
e) the abuse of material and human resources;

206 Published in the Romanian Official Gazette No. 1214 of December 17, 2004. Online access to the text of the Act: https://www.whistleblowing.it/Romanian%20Law%20571-2004%20-%20whistleblowingEN.pdf.
207 Dąbrowski, "Demaskacja," p. 43.
208 Wojciechowicz, "Sytuacja sygnalistów," p. 13.
209 R. Dimitriu, "Romania: First Steps to Whistleblowers' Protection," in: *Whistleblowing: A Comparative Study*, p. 246.

f) biased political activity by means of occupied office, except for people elected or appointed on political rules;
g) breaking of the law on access to information and transparency of decisions;
h) breaking of provisions concerning the public procurement and nonrefundable financing;
i) incompetence and negligence of responsibilities;
j) subjective evaluation of the personnel during the process of recruitment, selection, promotion, degradation, and dismissal;
k) breaking of administrative procedures or establishing internal procedures that are against the law;
l) issuing administrative acts or other acts in the interest of a particular group or a clientele;
m) flawed or fraudulent management of property of public authorities, public institutions, or other establishments provided in Article 2 of the Law;
n) breaking of other provisions issued in order to achieve the principle of good administration or to protect the public interest.

The provisions of the Act enable whistleblowers to choose the path of disclosing wrongdoings. It is possible to use any channel in all circumstances.[210] Their register was included in Article 6 of the Law No. 571/2004. Namely, it is possible to disclose information:

- directly to the supervisor of a person who broke the law;
- to the head of a public authority, institution, or budget unit, in which the person who violated the law is employed or in which an illegal practice was disclosed, even if the author of the disclosure cannot be identified;
- to a disciplinary committee or another similar body within the public authority;
- to judicial bodies;

210 Blueprint for Free Speech, "Gaps in the System: Whistleblower Laws in the EU," 2018, p. 15, https://www.changeofdirection.eu/assets/uploads/BLUEPRINT%20-%20Gaps%20in%20the%20System%20-%20Whistleblowers%20Laws%20in%20the%20EU.pdf, access: 26.08.2019.

- to bodies responsible for detecting and examining conflicts of interest and discrepancies;
- to a parliamentary committee;
- to the mass media;
- to professional bodies, trade unions, sector organizations; or
- non-governmental organizations.

However, the literature indicates that – despite the lack of indication of the order of using the abovementioned channels – the initial exhaustion of internal ways of disclosure seems to be an element that demonstrates the good faith of whistleblowers.[211] On the other hand, disclosing information about wrongdoings directly to the media – instead of the bodies proper for their resolution – may indicate the lack of whistleblowers' good faith.[212] The Law No. 571/2004 lists a number of principles of whistleblower protection in public interest. Among other things, the list includes the principle of liability, according to which the violation of law disclosed by whistleblowers must be supported by information or proofs concerning the committed act. On the other hand, the principle prohibiting the abuse of sanctions towards the person disclosing the violation of law constitutes that such a person cannot be submitted to unfair sanctions or be more severely penalized for other disciplinary misconducts. Whereas, the principle of good leadership constitutes that employees are encouraged to disclose in public interest in order to improve the administration potential and to increase the prestige of the public authorities, public institutions, and other entities specified in the Law No. 571/2004. The principle of good faith is also rather significant for whistleblowers, in accordance with which a person, who is an employee of public authorities, institutions, or another entity specified in the Law, and who discloses an action which constitutes a violation of rights, is guaranteed protection if they believe that such an action indeed occurred and that it was unlawful. The disclosure made in public interests uses the presumption of good faith unless it is disproved. Moreover, upon the request of the whistleblower, against whom began disciplinary proceedings as a result of the disclosure of information, the disciplinary committee or any similar

211 Dimitriu, "Romania: First Steps," p. 253.
212 Dimitriu, "Romania: First Steps," p. 253.

body within the organizational structure of the public authorities has the obligation to invite the press and a representative of a trade union or professional body. The disciplinary committee has the obligation to provide the whistleblower with protection by means of concealing their identity if any indicated person is their supervisor or has the power of control over the whistleblower. Moreover, if the whistleblower acted in good faith, the court may decide on the invalidity of the disciplinary or administrative sanctions applied towards them in the scope of retaliation actions undertaken due to his activity.

1.2.4 Slovenia

Slovenia has no act devoted exclusively to the protection of whistleblowers. Moreover, the provisions of the Slovenian labor law do not provide specific protection for people who disclose the perceived wrongdoings.[213] However, the protection of whistleblowers is inscribed in the anti-corruption activities of the state. The main act concerning the discussed issue is the Integrity and Prevention of Corruption Act of 2010.[214] This Act covers a broad scope of good manners recognized in the international arena in the field of whistleblower protection. Its provisions regulate such issues as the disclosure of wrongdoings, the guarantee of identity protection for whistleblowers, definitions of illegal and unethical actions or sanctions in a case of the violation of the whistleblower protection. This regulation does not provide the obligation to make disclosures of perceived wrongdoings nor the financial rewards for such actions.[215]

Article 1 of the Integrity and Prevention of Corruption Act establishes the means and methods for the purposes of strengthening integrity and

---

213 D. S. Peček, "Protection of Persons Reporting Corruption and Other Whistleblowers in the Republic of Slovenia," in: *Whistleblowing – A Comparative Study*, p. 263.

214 Official Gazette of the Republic of Slovenia No. 45/2010, 26/11 and 43/11. Online access to the text of the Act: https://publicofficialsfinancialdisclosure.worldbank.org/sites/fdl/files/assets/law-library-files/Slovenia_Integrity%20and%20the%20Prevention%20of%20Corruption%20Act_2010_en.pdf, access: 13.07.2019.

215 Peček, "Protection of Persons," p. 274.

transparency in order to prevent corruption and avoid and eliminate conflicts of interest. On the other hand, in accordance with Article 4 of the Act, "corruption" means any violation of the proper conduct of responsible officials in public or private sector – which also means the conduct of people who initiate such violations – or of people benefiting from the violation in order to gain undue, promised, offered, or transferred directly or indirectly benefits, or in order to gain undue, demanded, accepted, or expected benefits for own gain or for the gain of any other person.

Chapter III of the Act consists of regulations concerning the protection of people working in public and private sectors, who in good faith and in a reasonable way disclose their suspicions about illegal or unethical conducts, is crucial for the subject matter of the present study.[216] This chapter is composed of three articles, which concern the disclosure of corruption and the protection of disclosing people (Article 23), the disclosure of unethical and unlawful action (Article 24), or the means of protecting the disclosing person (Article 25).

No legal act in Slovenia includes a definition of whistleblowers. However, Article 23 of the discussed Act constitutes that every person may inform the Commission for the Prevention of Corruption[217] or another proper body about cases of corruption in the state office, within the local community, public authorities, or other legal entities subject to the public or private law, or about the conduct of a natural person in regard to which such a person thinks it contains elements of corruption. If the Commission recognizes that the disclosure contains elements of an offence prosecuted ex officio, it informs about it the proper law enforcement authorities. Upon the request of the disclosing person, the Commission and other proper authorities inform the disclosing person about the means or proceedings of actions undertaken in this matter.

The Commission for the Prevention of Corruption deals with the protection of not only whistleblowers, but also their disclosures.[218] Moreover, it

216 OECD (2016), *Committing*, p. 109.
217 See the website of the Commission for the Prevention of Corruption: https://www.kpk-rs.si/.
218 Annual reports from the proceedings of the Commission for the Prevention of Corruption for specific years are available at: www.kpk-rs.si/sl/komisija/letna-porocila.

ensures help for people who disclose perceived wrongdoings and monitors their activity and retaliatory actions against them. The legal status of the Commission for the Prevention of Corruption is regulated by Article 5 of the discussed Act, in accordance with which it is an autonomous and independent state body which – in order to strengthen the efficient functioning of legal state and to protect it from risks of corruptive practices – realizes its competences autonomously and fulfils its tasks determined in the Act and in other legal acts within and on the basis of proper legal provisions. What follows is that the Commission is not subjected to any ministry. Its main task is to protect the legal state from corruptive practices.[219] It has a wide scope of competences, among other things, the prevention and detection of corruption, violations of ethics and integrity principles in public offices. Moreover, the Commission has rights to access financial documents, pose questions to officials, or instruct various law enforcement authorities.[220] Thus, its main interests are activities in which there exists a suspicion that corruption or other wrongdoings do occur.

The Act regulates a number of protection means for whistleblowers, including identity protection. In accordance with Article 23 Paragraph 4 of the Act, the Commission will not reveal the identity of a disclosing person who prepared a report in good faith and truly believes the included information that will be evaluated by the Commission is true. However, if the disclosure was made anonymously, the identity of the whistleblower will not be determined if the abovementioned premises are fulfilled.[221] The court has the exclusive right to reveal the information and identity of whistleblowers if it is absolutely necessary for the protection of the public interest or rights of other people.[222] An attempt against the law to determine or reveal their identity is treated as an offence and is subject to penalty by fine.[223] In accordance with Article 77 Paragraph 2 Section 1 of

219 *The Commission for the Prevention of Corruption. An overview*, p. 2, https://publicofficialsfinancialdisclosure.worldbank.org/sites/fdl/files/assets/law-library-files/Slovenia_Integrity%20and%20the%20Prevention%20of%20Corruption%20Act_2010_en.pdf, access: 13.07.2019.

220 *The Commission for the Prevention*, p. 2.

221 Senčur Peček, "Protection of Persons," p. 265.

222 Article 23 Paragraph 8 of the Integrity and Prevention of Corruption Act.

223 Senčur Peček, "Protection of Persons," p. 265.

the Act, a person who – against the law – reveals the identity of a person, who made a report in good faith or in a reasonable way thought that the information was true, is subject to a fine of €1,000–2,000. However, for the sole attempt of determining the whistleblower's identity, there is a fine of €400–1,200 euros.[224] In turn, Article 77 Paragraph 6 of the Act states that a person responsible in a state or local body who has public authority or a legal entity of public or private law who violates the provisions of the Act by initiating proceedings to determine or reveal the whistleblower's identity due to the report, risks a fine of €400–4,000.[225]

If no feature of an offence is determined, the submission of a report in bad faith will be penalized on the basis of the present Act. Article 77 Paragraph 2 Section 1 of the Act constitutes that in a situation when the disclosure was made in bad faith and no feature of offence was determined, the whistleblower is subject to a fine of €1,000–2,000 euros. In turn Article 23 Paragraph 5 states that – when during the evaluation whether the report was made in good faith and the whistleblower truly believes that his information is true – the Commission will take into particular account the character and the seriousness of the disclosed practice, the risk of occurrence of detriment caused by this practice, the actual detriment which resulted from a potential violation of the obligation of the whistleblower to protect specific information, and the status of the body and person for whom the report was prepared.

Noteworthy, if the protection conditions for a whistleblower and his family are met in the context of the disclosure of corruption,[226] the Commission for the Prevention of Corruption may propose to the Commission for Witness Protection to put such people under the witness

---

224 Article 77 Paragraph 1 Section 3 of the Integrity and Prevention of Corruption Act.

225 In accordance with Article 78 of the Integrity and Prevention of Corruption Act, a person with public authority or any legal entity of public or private law who commits a minor offence, referred to, among others, in Article 77 Paragraph 6 of the present Act, is subjected to a fine of 400 to 100,000 euros, except for the Republic of Slovenia and local authorities.

226 In accordance with the Act on Witness Protection (*Zakon o zaščiti prič*), Official Gazette RS. No. 113/2005. 61/06 and 110/2007.

protection program or to the Attorney General to undertake immediate protection actions.[227]

In the discussed Act, the disclosure of other unethical or unlawful actions was regulated separately from cases of corruption disclosure. In accordance with Article 24 Paragraph 1 of the Act: "An official person who has reasonable grounds to believe that he has been requested to engage in illegal or unethical conduct, or has been subject to psychological or physical violence to that end, may report such practice to the superior or the person authorised by the superior (hereinafter: the responsible person)." Article 4 of the Act contains definitions of its terms, and so it explains that state officials are: officials, high-ranking officials, other state officials, managers and members of management, and supervisory boards of public sector entities.

In turn, Article 24 Paragraph 2 of the Act declares that the report specified in the previous paragraph and related to it procedure will be included in the scope of the Commission's competences if there is no responsible person, if the responsible person does not answer to the report in writing within the period of five business days, or if it is the responsible person who requests that a state official engage in illegal or unethical conduct. Next, the responsible person or the Commission will evaluate the actual situation on the basis of the received report, will give orders concerning further actions that must be undertaken if they are essential, and will undertake all essential actions to prevent illegal or unethical actions and their unfavorable consequences.[228]

Should the disclosure result in retaliation against the whistleblower, which has an unfavorable influence on him, they have the right to claim compensation from the employer for unlawful detriment. In accordance with Article 25 Paragraph 2 of the Act, the Commission for the Prevention of Corruption may offer the whistleblower its help in determining the causal connection between negative consequences and retaliation actions. After the determination of the occurrence of the above causal connection, the Commission may request from the employer an assurance that their

227 Article 23 Paragraph 6 of the Integrity and Prevention of Corruption Act.
228 Article 24 Paragraph 3 of the Integrity and Prevention of Corruption Act.

retaliatory actions will cease immediately.[229] What follows from the above, the Commission may play an important role in such cases, because without its help the employee may have difficulties in proving that the negative actions (e.g. mobbing) are the consequence of the disclosure e.g. of corruption.[230] The help of the Committee may be granted only when a legal dispute is initiated, and it ends after the dispute's final settlement.[231]

For causing detriment to whistleblowers or the sole undertaking of retaliatory actions against them, a person responsible on the part of state or local authority bodies, people with public authority, or other legal entities subject to public or private law is subject to a fine of €400–4,000.[232] In turn, the employer, except for the Republic of Slovenia and local authorities, is subject for the above actions to a fine of €400–100,000.[233] The same penalties are applied in the case of noncompliance to the request of the Commission concerning the immediate cessation of retaliatory actions against whistleblowers.

Moreover, the provisions of the Act enable whistleblowers who are state officials the submission of a transfer request to another, equal position.[234] It is possible in a situation when – despite the above request of the Committee – the retaliatory actions against the employee did not cease and they prevent the employee from continuing work in the current position. Such a request for the transfer of the employee is related to the obligation of the employer to inform the Commission about the actions undertaken to complete it. Pursuant to Article 25 Paragraph 6 of the Act, the employer of a public official has up to ninety days to transfer the employee to another, equal position. If the employer fails to do so without providing justified reasons, they are subject to a fine. For people responsible on the part of the employer, the fine equals €400–4,000,[235] while in the case of the employer it equals €400–100,000 euros, except for the Republic of Slovenia and local

229 Article 25 Paragraph 3 of the Integrity and Prevention of Corruption Act.
230 Peček, "Protection of Persons," p. 268.
231 K-Monitor Association and Hungarian Civil Liberties Union, "Final study," http://www.whistleblowing-cee.org/summing-study/, access: 13.07.2019.
232 Article 77 Paragraph 7 of the Integrity and Prevention of Corruption Act.
233 Article 78 of the Integrity and Prevention of Corruption Act.
234 Article 25 Paragraph 4 of the Integrity and Prevention of Corruption Act.
235 Article 77 Paragraph 9 of the Integrity and Prevention of Corruption Act.

authorities.[236] Let us emphasize that only employees who are state officials may submit transfer requests.[237]

In accordance with the provisions of the Act, the employer must prove that all measures undertaken against the whistleblower were not related to his disclosure of wrongdoings; i.e. that they did not have a retaliatory character.[238]

1.2.5 Ireland

The main legal act that guarantees the protection of whistleblowers in Ireland is the Protected Disclosures Act of July 8, 2014.[239] Often called "the Whistleblowers Act," it entered into force on July 15, 2014. The decision for its creation and the pace of legislative work were influenced by a number of political and economic events,[240] such as controversies regarding the disclosure of wrongdoings in An Garda Síochána – the Irish police service – which led to such actions as the resignation of the then Ireland's Minister for Justice and Equality and the Garda Commissioner.[241] The Act was a breakthrough in the Irish law, as it constituted the first attempt at a comprehensive coverage of the protection of people who disclose the cases of malpractices at work in a single document.[242] The literature indicates that – before its adoption – the protection of whistleblowers in Ireland was merely fragmentary and contained loopholes.[243]

The objective of the Act was the creation of an environment in which employees of the public, private, and noncommercial sectors may disclose

236 Article 78 of the Integrity and Prevention of Corruption Act.

237 Peček, "Protection of Persons," p. 274.

238 Article 25 Paragraph 5 of the Integrity and Prevention of Corruption Act.

239 The text of the Act is accessible online at: http://www.irishstatutebook.ie/eli/2014/act/14/enacted/en/html.

240 Department of Public Expenditure and Reform, *Statutory Review of the Protected Disclosures Act 2014*, 2018, p. 6, https://assets.gov.ie/8765/7e1f2c66e7c04062a25561a848e17943.pdf, access: 25.07.2019.

241 Wikipedia. The Free Encyclopedia, "Garda whistleblower scandal," https://en.wikipedia.org/wiki/Garda_whistleblower_scandal, access: 11.09.2019.

242 OECD (2016), *Committing to*, p. 171.

243 M. Doherty and D. Ryan, "Whistleblowing: National Report for Ireland" in: *Whistleblowing – A Comparative Study*, p. 181.

malpractices[244] without fear of retaliation from the employer or a third party.[245] Therefore, the provisions provide a number of protection measures for whistleblowers.

The Act provides protection for employees of public, private, and non-profit sectors. Its definition of the term "worker" has a very broad meaning. In accordance with Article 3 of the Act, which explains the terms used in its contents, a "worker" means a person who:

(a) is an employee;
(b) entered into or works or worked under any other contract, whether express or implied and (if it is express) whether oral or in writing, whereby the individual undertook to do or perform (whether personally or otherwise) any work or services for another party to the contract for the purposes of that party's business;
(c) works or worked for a person in circumstances in which:
  (i) the individual is introduced or supplied to do the work by a third person; and
  (ii) the terms on which the individual is engaged to do the work are or were in practice substantially determined not by the individual but by the person for whom the individual works or worked, by the third person or by both of them;

  or
(d) is or was provided with work experience pursuant to a training course or programme or with training for employment (or with both) otherwise than:
  (i) under a contract of employment; or
  (ii) by an educational establishment on a course provided by the establishment, and includes an individual who is deemed to be a worker by virtue of subsection (2) (b) and any reference to a worker being employed or to employment shall be construed accordingly.

244 In accordance with Article 5 Paragraph 3 of the Protected Disclosures Act.
245 Department of Public Expenditure and Reform, *Statutory Review*, p. 1, https://assets.gov.ie/8765/7e1f2c66e7c04062a25561a848e17943.pdf, access: 13.07.2019.

Moreover, for the purposes of the Act every person who is or was a member of Garda Síochána or "a civil servant is deemed to be an employee and an individual who is or was a member of the Permanent Defence Force or the Reserve Defence Force is deemed to be a worker."[246]

We should mention here Article 13 of the Act, which constitutes that, "If a person causes detriment to another person because the other person or a third person made a protected disclosure, the person to whom the detriment is caused has a right of action in tort against the person by whom the detriment is caused." Thus, the above fragment provides protection not only for the employee but also e.g. for people who encourage others to make disclosures or confirm disclosures made by whistleblowers.[247]

In turn, Article 5 of the Act defines which types of information disclosure receive protection. Above all, it must concern "relevant information." It may be considered as such if an employee demonstrates with reasonable belief one or more relevant wrongdoings, and the employee obtains the information due to the situation of employment. In accordance with Paragraph 7 of the indicated Article, the motivation of a whistleblower does not matter from the viewpoint of protection. Such an attitude has the objective of encouraging whistleblowers to act by means of eliminating as many discouraging elements as possible. Moreover, the protection of whistleblowers disregards whether the disclosed information will eventually reveal the existence of wrongdoings. However, intentionally false disclosures are excluded from protection, because they do not meet the criterion of "reasonable belief."[248]

In accordance with Article 5 Paragraph 3 of the Act, the relevant wrongdoings are:

(a) that an offence has been, is being or is likely to be committed;
(b) that a person has failed, is failing or is likely to fail to comply with any legal obligation, other than one arising under the worker's contract of employment or other contract whereby the worker undertakes to do or perform personally any work or services;

---

246 Article 3 of the Protected Disclosures Act.
247 Doherty and Ryan, "Whistleblowing: National Report for Ireland," p. 183.
248 Doherty and Ryan, "Whistleblowing: National Report for Ireland," p. 184.

(c) that a miscarriage of justice has occurred, is occurring or is likely to occur;
(d) that the health or safety of any individual has been, is being or is likely to be endangered;
(e) that the environment has been, is being or is likely to be damaged;
(f) that an unlawful or otherwise improper use of funds or resources of a public body, or of other public money, has occurred, is occurring or is likely to occur;
(g) that an act or omission by or on behalf of a public body is oppressive, discriminatory or grossly negligent or constitutes gross mismanagement; or
(h) that information tending to show any matter falling within any of the preceding paragraphs has been, is being or is likely to be concealed or destroyed.

The listed wrongdoings may take place in Ireland and abroad.

The Act provides a multilevel ("gradual") system of wrongdoing disclosure. Even though there is no legal requirement for whistleblowers to disclose information firstly in their workplace, the legislator encourages them to do so by requiring the fulfilment of additional conditions in the case of disclosures through other channels.

In accordance with Article 6 Paragraph 1 of the Act, a whistleblower may disclose wrongdoings to the employer or other responsible person. The "worker" is permitted to disclose to a responsible person where the worker reasonably believes that this person has legal responsibility for the relevant wrongdoing or the wrongdoing does not relates solely or mainly to the "worker's" employer.[249] This is an internal path whose use requires only the reasonable belief of the whistleblower that the disclosed wrongdoings actually occurred.

Moreover, a person who is or was employed in a public institution may disclose protected information to a proper minister.[250] In this case, the proof

249 Doherty and Ryan, "Whistleblowing: National Report for Ireland," p. 184.
250 Department of Public Expenditure and Reform, *Statutory Review*, p. 7, https://assets.gov.ie/8765/7e1f2c66e7c04062a25561a848e17943.pdf, access: 13.07.2019.

criteria for the disclosure of information are the same as those that are applied to the internal disclosure to the employer, i.e. an employee must have justified reasons to believe that the disclosure of information concerns law violation or a possibility of the occurrence of such violation.

The disclosure of wrongdoings may also be made to prescribed persons. These include specific bodies,[251] which may receive disclosures connected to the activity they monitor and regulate.[252] On account of their role, these bodies may be a proper place for the reception and examination of issues disclosed by whistleblowers. Such bodies are, among others, the Central Bank of Ireland, the Health and Safety Authority, and the Data Protection Commission.[253] Pursuant to Article 7 of the Act, the disclosure of wrongdoings to a specific body will be protected, if a whistleblower has reasonable belief that a given malpractice is within the competences of the specific body and the information that he discloses and all included allegations are substantially true; i.e. it is a higher standard than that required in the case of disclosing wrongdoings to the employer.

In accordance with Article 9 of the Act, a "worker" may also make a protected disclosure of information during the reception of legal advice from a lawyer, attorney-at-law, representative of a trade union, or an official of a statutory body.

After fulfilling conditions specified in the Act, the protected disclosure may also be made in a different manner than indicated above, i.e. by means of disclosing information to an external person, e.g. a representative of the media.[254] To receive protection, an employee must have reasonable belief

---

251 Listed in SI 339/2014 (http://www.irishstatutebook.ie/eli/2014/si/339/made/en/print), amended SI 448/2015 (http://www.irishstatutebook.ie/eli/2015/si/448/made/en/print) and S.I. 490/2016 (http://www.irishstatutebook.ie/eli/2016/si/490/made/en/print).

252 Department of Public Expenditure and Reform, *Statutory Review*, p. 4 9, https://assets.gov.ie/8765/7e1f2c66e7c04062a25561a848e17943.pdf, access: 13.07.2019.

253 Citizens Information, "Protection for whistleblowers," https://www.citizensinformation.ie/en/employment/enforcement_and_redress/protection_for_whistleblowers.html, access: 24.07.2019.

254 Department of Public Expenditure and Reform, *Statutory Review*, p. 7, https://assets.gov.ie/8765/7e1f2c66e7c04062a25561a848e17943.pdf, access: 13.07.2019.

that the disclosed information and all included allegations are substantially true and – taking into account all circumstances of the issue – that the disclosure of information is reasonable. Pursuant to Article 10 Paragraph 3 of the Act, in order to confirm the above, one must take into account in particular:

(a) the identity of the person to whom the disclosure is made;
(b) … the seriousness of the relevant wrongdoing;
(c) … whether the relevant wrongdoing is continuing or is likely to occur in the future;
(d) … any action which the employer of the worker or the person to whom the previous disclosure was made has taken or might reasonably be expected to have taken as a result of the previous disclosure; and
(e) … whether in making the disclosure to the employer the worker complied with any procedure the use of which by the worker was authorised by the employer.

Moreover, to make a protected disclosure in the discussed mode, the objective cannot be personal gain. Furthermore, at least one of the conditions listed in Article 10 Paragraph 2 of the Act must be met:

(a) that, at the time the worker makes the disclosure, the worker reasonably believes that the worker will be subjected to penalisation by the worker's employer if the worker makes a disclosure …;
(b) that, in a case where no relevant person is prescribed … in relation to the relevant wrongdoing, the worker reasonably believes that it is likely that evidence relating to the relevant wrongdoing will be concealed or destroyed if the worker makes a disclosure …;
(c) that the worker has previously made a disclosure of substantially the same information …;
(d) that the relevant wrongdoing is of an exceptionally serious nature.

The Act provides protection for people who disclose wrongdoings about which they learned due to their employment. The literature indicates that the Protected Disclosures Act changed the Unfair Dismissals Acts of 1977[255] in several significant aspects.[256]

---

255 The text of the Act is accessible online at: http://www.irishstatutebook.ie/eli/1977/act/10/enacted/en/html.

256 Doherty and Ryan, "Whistleblowing: National Report for Ireland," p. 185.

Above all, we should emphasize that the dismissal of an employee which in consequence of their protected disclosure is considered unfair. A whistleblower dismissed for such action, despite following the provisions of the Protected Disclosures Act, may receive compensation in a maximal amount of up to five-years-worth of remuneration; the maximal amount of compensation in other cases concerning unfair dismissal is limited to a two-year remuneration.[257] Just as in the case of every unfair dismissal, in this case the sued employer must provide proof. It means that it is the obligation of the employer to prove that there were reasonable premises to dismiss the employee, unrelated to their protected disclosure. Moreover, we should indicate that the protection from an unfair dismissal is substantially applied to employees with more than one year of experience, although this limitation is not applicable in cases of dismissal due to the submission of protected disclosure.[258]

The Protected Disclosures Act also provides protection for whistleblowers from other types of retaliation from the employer. Article 12 Paragraph 1 of the Act constitutes that – in the case of a protected disclosure – the employer cannot punish or threat to punish the employee, encourage it, or allow other people to do so. Article 3 of the Act indicates that "punishment" means every action or negligence which causes detriment to the employee, e.g. suspension, dismissal, degradation, deprivation of promotion opportunities, reduction of remuneration, initiation of disciplinary proceedings, reprimanding, or application of another penalty – including a financial one – coercion, intimidation, harassment, discrimination, or a threat of retaliation. Should any of the above occur, the employee may also receive compensation of up to five-years-worth of remuneration.[259]

Moreover, Article 13 of the Act provides the right of action in tort regarding every detriment suffered due to the submission of a protected

257 Doherty and Ryan, "Whistleblowing: National Report for Ireland," p. 186.

258 Department of Public Expenditure and Reform, *Statutory Review*, p. 7, https://assets.gov.ie/8765/7e1f2c66e7c04062a25561a848e17943.pdf, access: 13.07.2019.

259 Doherty and Ryan, "Whistleblowing: National Report for Ireland," p. 186.

disclosure. In Paragraph 3, detriment is defined as: coercion, intimidation, or harassment; disadvantage or adverse treatment in relation to employment (or prospective employment); injury, damage or loss; and threat of retaliation.

Noteworthy, the amount of fair and just compensation in the case in which an inquiry of a relevant offence was not the only or main motivation for the information disclosure, may be up to 25 % lower than the amount of compensation due in other cases.

The provisions of the Protected Disclosures Act protect the identity of whistleblowers. In accordance with Article 16 Paragraph 1 of the Act, a person to whom information is disclosed by means of a protected disclosure and every person to whom information is disclosed in such a manner from the former person in the scope of their responsibilities, is obligated to keep in secrecy all information that may reveal the identity of the whistleblower. Hence, there is an obligation that the recipients of disclosed information to undertake all reasonable steps in order to protect the identity of the whistleblower and ensure that the information is treated as confidential. However, there are some exceptions to this rule. The above will not apply in a number of cases indicated in the Act, e.g. if a disclosure of information is essential to the public interest or is required by law. Let us add that the disclosure may be made anonymously, though it may significantly hamper the effective reaction of a proper entity.

1.2.6. Italy

The increasing number of legal regulations concerning the protection of whistleblowers worldwide also influenced Italy. In 2012, Italy passed the Anti-Corruption Law 190/2012,[260] whose main goal was to improve transparency in the public sector. The Law contains regulations for the protection of whistleblowers. Among other things, the Law introduces obligation for public administration bodies and state enterprises to adopt internal measures for the protection of whistleblowers. The application of its provisions

260 The complete text of the Law is available online at https://www.gazzettaufficiale.it/eli/id/2012/11/13/012G0213/sg. Later referred to as the Law 190/2012.

is limited, as they only concern persons employed in the public sector, which causes a significant gap in the protection of whistleblowers.

The situation changed with the introduction of Law 179/2017 of November 30, 2017, which entered into force on December 29, 2017.[261] Its aim was to strengthen the protection of whistleblowers in the public sector and to introduce protection measures for private sector whistleblowers. The new rules extended the scope of the existing regulations for the protection of civil servants to include employees of public enterprises and public sector entities, and also private sector entities which supply the public sector. The main change introduced by the Law 179/2017 was the regulation of employers' obligations concerning the implementation of a whistleblowing system. The provisions of the Law slightly differ in relation to the public and private sectors, which this work discusses in more detail below.

As mentioned, the amendments also apply to private companies, namely those that decided to implement an advanced compliance program for the prevention of criminal offenses, in accordance with the Legislative Decree 231/2001 of June 8, 2001.[262] An effective implementation of this program may exempt a company from liability for offenses committed by its CEOs, employees, or external partners in the interest of the company.

Previously, the protection of whistleblowers in Italy in the private sector was limited and only result from the implementation of EU regulations.[263] The Decree's entry into force was intended to encourage the private sector to adopt specific internal compliance programs. However, one of the significant shortcomings of the Decree 231/2001 was that it did not ensure the protection of whistleblowers. The provisions of the Decree 231/2001 were supplemented in this respect by Law 179/2017. The latter applies to

261 The complete text of the Law is available online at https://static1.squarespace.com/static/5a742d5ae9bfdf1f3304898d/t/5a974db8419202f909ee4e01/1519865278761/Italy+WBer+Law+-+2017+English.pdf. Later referred to as the Law 179/2017.

262 The complete text of the Law is available online at https://sherloc.unodc.org/res/cld/document/legislative-decree-8-6-2001-n-231_html/Legislative_Decree_8-6-2001_n_231_EN.pdf. Later referred to as Law 231/2001.

263 We must mention in this respect such EU Directives as: 2013/36/EU, 2015/849/EU, 2016/1034/EU, which obligate financial institutions and insurance companies to implement infringement reporting procedures.

companies that implemented a compliance model based on the provisions of the Decree 231/2001, which provides further obligations for these companies.

According to Article 1(1) of the Law 179/2017, a whistleblower in the public sector is a person who – in the interest of public administration – reports information about illegal conduct of which they became aware in connection with their employment. A whistleblower may be any employee employed in public administration. These protection measures are also extended to employees of private companies under public control (it. *societá private sotto il controllo pubblico*) and public economic entities (it. *enti pubblici economici*), and also all employees and associates of private companies who work or supply products and services to public entities. In the latter case, the protection covers whistleblowers who are not part of the public administration, but who – by virtue of their work – have access to information that may be the subject of their report. We should note that each of these companies must adopt or amend its whistleblowing policy to comply with statutory requirements.

Informers can report detected violations to the Transparency and Anticorruption Officer, the National Anticorruption Agency (ANAC), directly to the judiciary authority, or the accountant as the fiscal authority.

The provisions of Law 179/2017 stipulate that – after lodging a report – a whistleblower shall not be the subject of retaliation through imposition of any sanctions, dismissal, demotion, transfer to another office, or any other measures that directly or indirectly impact their working conditions negatively. If a whistleblower is dismissed for their actions, they have the right to demand reinstatement, compensation for the damage suffered, and payment of social security contributions due for the period between their dismissal and reinstatement. An employer who wishes to discharge oneself of the liability must prove that the measures against the whistleblower were not retaliatory or discriminatory and have no relation to the whistleblower's disclosure of irregularities. We should emphasize that the above protection is not absolute and does not apply to persons whose reports are defamatory or libelous. The aim of this provision is to prevent abuse of the whistleblowing system. The Law 179/2017 also provides the protection of the whistleblower's identity, which may nevertheless be disclosed as part of a criminal trial.

Moreover, we must note that Article 1(6) of the Law 179/2017 provides the possibility that ANAC will impose sanctions of €5,000–30,000 on the entities responsible for retaliatory measures against the whistleblower, and €10,000–50,000 if ANAC finds that there is no internal system for reporting irregularities or that no appropriate measures were taken as a result of the whistleblower's report.

The Law 179/2017 is a substantial amendment to Decree 231/2001 on the criminal liability of private-sector operators. As already mentioned above, the effective implementation of a protection mechanism for whistleblowers can exempt the company from liability for offenses committed by its CEOs, employees, or external partners in the interest of the company.

The Law 179/2017 requires private entities with already established compliance programs to introduce irregularity reporting systems for whistleblowers. Moreover, the Law 179/2017 specifies the requirements that these systems should meet. In particular, according to Article 2 Paragraph 2-bis(a), such a mechanism must provide one or more channels for employees to internally report irregularities. We should highlight that the whistleblower must base their allegations on "precise and coherent factual elements." Moreover, the companies should implement at least one alternative reporting channel to guarantee confidentiality of the whistleblower's identity. Once a report is lodged, these channels should protect the identity of the whistleblower and the confidentiality of the information transmitted.

The law further provides a prohibition of direct or indirect retaliation or discrimination against whistleblowers following their report; e.g. such an employee may not be dismissed or transferred to another post. Article 2 Paragraph 2-quarter states that discriminatory or retaliatory dismissals, changes in duty, or any other retaliatory or discriminatory action against the whistleblower are null and void. It is the responsibility of the employer to prove that the measures taken are justified, for reasons other than the whistleblower's disclosure of irregularities.

Furthermore, the Law 179/2017 imposes an obligation to enforce sanctions, both against persons who retaliate against whistleblowers and against those whistleblowers who file unsubstantiated complaints intentionally or as a result of gross negligence. According to Article 2 Paragraph 2-ter of the Law, discriminatory measures against whistleblowers may be the subject of an individual's or a competent trade union's report to the National Labor Inspectorate (it. *Ispettorato del Lavoro*).

1.2.7 France

After a long support campaign from NGOs, the French legislators decided to create a protective legal framework for whistleblowers. On December 9, 2016, the Law No. 2016–1691 on transparency, fight against corruption, and economic modernization[264] was passed – the so-called Sapin II Law[265] – and entered into force on June 1, 2017. This regulation is a legal instrument for combating corruption and contains provisions relating to the activity of whistleblowers.[266]

The provisions of the Law impose an obligation to implement whistleblowing procedures on public and private entities that employ at least fifty employees, state administration offices, municipalities with more than 10,000 inhabitants, and also public inter-municipal cooperation institutions with own taxation, departments, and regions. These must have the possibility to enable information sharing by employees and by external and occasional business partners. Entities with fewer than fifty employees are not obligated to implement this procedure but can do so on a voluntary basis. The details of this obligation are laid down in Decree 2017-564 of April 19, 2017,[267] which entered into force on January 1, 2018.

The Sapin II Law contains the definition of a "whistleblower." According to Article 6, a whistleblower is "an individual who discloses or reports, selflessly and in good faith, an offense or misdemeanor, a serious

---

264 The complete text of the Law is available online at https://www.legifrance.gouv.fr/affichTexte.do?cidTexte=JORFTEXT000033558528&dateTexte=20170616. Later referred to as Sapin II Law.

265 This commonly used term comes from the name of the Minister of Economy and Finance, Michel Sapin, who presented its draft version.

266 J. Meijers, *The Protection of Whistleblowers. Challenges and Opportunities for Local and Regional Government*, Governance Committee, 2019, p. 14, https://rm.coe.int/the-protection-of-whistleblowers-challenges-and-opportunities-for-loca/16809312bd, access: 06.08.2019.

267 The complete text of the Law is available online at https://www.legifrance.gouv.fr/affichTexte.do?cidTexte=JORFTEXT000034443268&categorieLien=id.

and clear breach of an international obligation ratified or approved by France, a unilateral act of an international organization adopted on the basis of such an obligation, right or regulation, or a serious threat to, or damage to, public interest, of which he or she has become aware." As mentioned above, only individuals can be considered whistleblowers. Legal persons may also notify the relevant entities of abuses, but such informants will not benefit from legal protection provided by this law. The whistleblower must report irregularities in good faith, i.e. they must have sufficient grounds to believe that the information they provide is true. Moreover, the Sapin II Law emphasize that the whistleblower should act in a selfless manner by only taking into account public interest. This principle clearly rejects e.g. the US approach, where certain legal acts – like the Dodd-Frank Act – allow whistleblowers to receive remuneration for disclosing irregularities.

The law imposes certain restrictions on the scope of information that whistleblowers can report. Namely, facts, information, or documents, regardless of their form and medium, covered by the obligation to maintain national secrecy, medical confidentiality, or professional lawyer-client secrecy, are excluded from the scope of the reporting system.

The procedures for reporting infringements and threats should indicate to potential whistleblowers the method of providing information and the scope of information that they can report.[268] Moreover, these procedures should provide the following routine operations:

(a) immediately informing the whistleblower that his or her report has been received, giving a reasonable and foreseeable time for its examination, and indicating how they will be informed of the action taken;
(b) ensuring strict confidentiality of the identity of the whistleblower, reported facts, and persons concerned; and
(c) destroying elements of the report, which could enable the identification of the whistleblower or persons concerned; in cases in which no action was taken or two months elapsed since all admissibility or verification procedures were completed.

268 Hryniewicz, Krak, *Sygnaliści*, p. 46.

To benefit from the protective measures provided by the Sapin II Law, the whistleblower must operate according to its reporting system. In this respect, Article 8 of the Law provides a specific three-step procedure. The first recipient of the report must be the direct or indirect superior of the informer: the employer or a person designated by the employer (*référent*). If this person takes no action to verify the admissibility of the report within a reasonable period of time, the whistleblower may refer the matter to a judicial, administrative, or professional organization body (second stage of the procedure). As a last resort, if the abovementioned authorities do not examine the report within three months, the whistleblower may disclose the information to the public (third stage of the procedure). The rules allow whistleblowers to submit a report without completing the first stage in the event of a serious and imminent threat or risk of irreparable harm.

Article 9 (I) of the Sapin II Law stipulates that the reporting procedures shall ensure strict confidentiality of the identity of the whistleblower, the facts, and the persons concerned. Information that would allow one to establish the identity of the whistleblower may be disclosed only upon the whistleblower's consent. One exception is the disclosure of these data to judicial authorities. While providing full confidentiality for the whistleblower's identity and simultaneously enabling judicial authorities to obtain information on the subject whenever necessary, the rules ensure an appropriate balance between protecting the confidentiality of whistleblowers and the possibility of a fair trial. According to Article 9 (II) of the Law, the above disclosure of the confidential information may result in a sentence of two years' imprisonment and a fine of €30,000.

Employees who disclose perceived irregularities benefit from special protection against any retaliatory or discriminatory measures in the workplace. According to Article 10 of the Sapin II Law, a person who lodged a report under its provisions cannot be excluded from participation in the recruitment procedure on that basis and cannot be refused access to internships and traineeships. Furthermore, employers shall not penalize, dismiss, or discriminate against any worker on the grounds of their report, especially in regard to salary, incentives, shareholdings, training, reclassification, division of duties, qualification, classification, promotion opportunities, or contract extension. Consequently, any decision or action against an employee in breach of the above provisions is invalid. The Sapin II Law also provides the burden of proof to be shifted to the employee's benefit, should there arise a dispute between the employee and the employer as a result of the above forms of retaliation. In such a situation, it is the defendant employer who must prove justification for their action by an objective reason unrelated to the reporting of irregularities by the informant.

In order to ensure effective protection, the Sapin II Law creates the possibility of imposing sanctions on individuals who in any way hinder the whistleblower's report of irregularities. In this respect, Article 13 of the Sapin II Law provides a penalty of up to one year of imprisonment and a fine of €15,000.

However, we must indicate that the whistleblower's failure to comply with the provisions of the Law, but also with the internal procedures e.g. specifically introduced in the workplace, should generally inhibit the use of the legal protection system. The whistleblower's failure to comply with the Sapin II Law may constitute a basis for their employee's liability e.g. dismissal, civil liability e.g. for damage caused, or even criminal liability.

1.2.8 Other Selected States

For the purpose of the present study, I detailed above the regulations concerning the protection of whistleblowers only for certain countries. However, let us note that the legislation of many other countries also provides regulations to the matter in question.

For example, Australia has regulations on the protection of whistleblowers for many years. However, these regulations differ between individual states.[269] Legal solutions in Australia were gradually introduced over several years, due to the country's internal conditions.[270] The first legal act was the Whistleblowers Protection Act of 1993 in the state of South Australia.[271] In the following years, legal acts that regulate the protection in the field of whistleblowing[272] were successively created at the state level. At the federal

269 J. J. Wojciechowicz, "Sytuacja sygnalistów," p. 12.

270 Dąbrowski, "Demaskacja," p. 42.

271 J. J. Wojciechowicz, *Rozwiązania australijskie w zakresie ochrony whistleblowerów*, 2009, http://www.batory.org.pl/doc/Australia_prezentacja_30032009.pdf., access: 24.07.2019.

272 Wojciechowicz, "Sytuacja sygnalistów," p. 12.

level, the Public Interest Disclosure Bill was created in 2001, followed by the Public Interest Disclosure Act,[273] which introduced solutions for the public sector in 2013. On February 19, 2019, the Australian Parliament adopted a reform of the legislation on whistleblowers in the form of the Treasury Laws Amendment (Enhancing Whistleblower Protections) Act of 2019,[274] which aimed to protect whistleblowers and provide serious civil and criminal sanctions.

Slovakia introduced the protection of whistleblowers in the Act of October 16, 2014, on Methods of Reporting Actions against Society and on Amendments to Certain Laws, passed by the National Council of the Slovak Republic.[275] The aim of the Act is to safeguard the rights of employees who decide to report – in good faith – behaviors that threaten public interest, while ensuring that they do not become victims of retaliatory measures.[276] The legislation on the protection of whistleblowers in Slovakia was amended as of March 1, 2019. The Act of 2014 was repealed in its entirety and replaced by Act 54/2019 on the Protection of Persons who Report Actions against Society and on Amendments to Certain Laws. Its purpose was to strengthen and increase the effectiveness of the protection provided by the previous regulation. The regulations of the Act 54/2019 expand the scope of protection of whistleblowers and establish a new supervisory authority for the protection of whistleblowers. They also introduce new obligations for whistleblowing and strengthen the ones existing for employers.

---

273 The complete text of the Act is available online at https://www.legislation.gov.au/Details/C2019C00026.

274 The complete text of the Act is available online at https://www.legislation.gov.au/Details/C2019A00010.

275 *Słow. Zakon zo 16. oktobra 2014 o niektórych opatreniach súvisiacich z oznamovanim protispoločenskej činnosti a o zmene a doplnení niektorých zákonov*. The complete text of the Act is available online at http://www.reming.sk/files/2015-07-22-075206-z__kon_307_2014.pdf.

276 M. Waszak, "Status osób ujawniających nieprawidłowości w miejscu pracy w Republice Słowackiej i jego ewolucja z perspektywy przepisów ustawy z dnia 16 października 2014 roku," *Zarządzanie Publiczne* 4(40)/ 2017, Wydawnictwo Uniwersytetu Jagiellońskiego, Kraków, p. 552.

In the Netherlands, the Whistleblowers Authority Act[277] came into force on July 1, 2016, and established *Huis voor klokkenluiders* – the institution that receives reports on irregularities. Among other things, the Whistleblowers Authority Act obligates all entities in the Netherlands with more than fifty employees to implement an internal whistleblower reporting procedure and prohibits retaliation against whistleblowers. However, the literature highlights the shortcomings of this regulation, including penalties for those who retaliate against whistleblowers and measures to compensate for their losses as a result of their actions.[278]

Moreover, there are present comprehensive legal solutions that protect whistleblowers in Sweden, Malta, Hungary, Malta, New Zealand, South Africa, Japan, India, South Korea, Ghana, Uganda, and Jamaica.[279]

1.3 Whistleblower Protection in the Jurisprudence of the European Court of Human Rights

In order to achieve the goals of this study, we should scrutinize the jurisprudence of the European Court of Human Rights (ECHR), which shapes the understanding of human rights in Poland. A number of rulings of the ECHR determined the scope of freedom of expression of persons who report irregularities in the workplace. The literature indicates that the ECHR case law may be useful in cases before Polish courts, because it is binding for these courts, while their failure to comply with it exposes the state to liability for damages.[280]

The ECHR examined the activities of whistleblowers in the context of the protection of freedom of expression. It considered whether whistleblowers may invoke the freedom of expression – in this case freedom of information[281] – under Article 10 of the European Convention for the Protection of

---

277 The complete text of the Act is available online at https://huisvoorklokkenluiders.nl/wp-content/uploads/2018/01/20160803_Wet-_Engelse-versie_BZK116131.pdf.

278 Wojciechowicz, "Sytuacja sygnalistów," p. 13.

279 Waszak, "Status osób ujawniających," p. 554.

280 Głowacka, Ploszka, Sczaniecki, *Wiem*, p. 17.

281 I. Kondak, "Wolność pracowników do wyrażania opinii na gruncie orzecznictwa Europejskiego Trybunału Praw Człowieka," in: *Prawo do godnego życia w świetle Europejskiej Konwencji Praw Człowieka i innych*

Human Rights and Fundamental Freedoms.[282] Article 10 Paragraph 1 of the Convention stipulates that, "Everyone has the right to freedom of expression. This right shall include freedom to hold opinions and to receive and impart information and ideas without interference by public authority and regardless of frontiers." However, this provision is not absolute.[283] Article 10 Paragraph 2 explains that the said freedom may be subject to limitations and sanctions, as provided by law and necessary in a democratic society, for the protection of the reputation and rights of others and for the protection of confidential information, among other things.

Freedom of expression, since everyone is entitled to it, therefore also applies to workers, regardless of their status, form of work or sector of employment.[284] However, the ECHR has underscored in its case law that this freedom is subject to certain restrictions in the workplace. When exercising this freedom, employees must bear in mind their obligations towards the employer, such as the duty of loyalty, restraint, and discretion.

As already indicated in previous parts of the study, a particularly high degree of loyalty may be required of civil servants[285] or officers of uniformed services,[286] but in certain situations these functionaries should also benefit from protection against the negative consequences of reporting irregularities. We should also note that in some professions a lower degree of loyalty is required, e.g. from journalists.[287] Due to the nature of their profession,

---

standardów międzynarodowych, Ministerstwo Spraw Zagranicznych – Departament do Spraw Postępowań przed Międzynarodowymi Organami Ochrony Praw Człowieka, Warszawa 2018, p. 53.

282 *Convention for the Protection of Human Rights and Fundamental Freedoms drew up by the Council of Europe and signed on November 4, 1950*; *Dziennik Ustaw* 61.284/1993.

283 Kondak, "Wolność," p. 49.

284 Kondak, "Wolność," p. 49.

285 Ruling of 17.11.2016, Karapetyan and Others v. Armenia, complaint No. 59001/08 concerning the dismissal of senior officials of the Ministry of Foreign Affairs due to them publicly stating that the presidential elections were fraudulent.

286 ECHR ruling of November 25, 1997, in Grigoriades v. Greece, complaint No. 24348/94; ECHR ruling of May 20, 1999 in Recveni v. Hungary, complaint No. 24348/94. See also ECHR ruling of January 8, 2013, in Bucur and Tom v. Romania, complaint No. 40238/02, described in Chapter Three.

287 Głowacka, Ploszka, Sczaniecki, *Wiem*, p. 23.

they have the right – or even duty – to comment on matters of public interest.[288]

In the context of whistleblower activities, the rulings of the ECHR in Guja v. Moldova[289] and Heinisch v. Germany[290] are particularly important, as they set criteria for assessing whether a worker can be considered a whistleblower.[291]

First, we should mention the ruling of February 12, 2008, in Guja v. Moldova,[292] in which the ECHR referred for the first time to the activities of whistleblowers. This ruling introduces a conventional concept for the protection of whistleblowers. In this case, an official from the Moldovan Prosecutor's Office provided information on the influence of politicians on the prosecution's activities. In response, the ECHR concluded that persons employed in the public sector by virtue of their function may possess information – including confidential information – whose disclosure would serve public interest.[293] Moreover, the proceedings found that an employee who reports information may benefit from protection by meeting certain criteria:

- in the first instance, the whistleblower benefits from another effective means of providing an adequate response to the breach to be disclosed; if any such means exist;
- the disclosure serves public interest;
- the disclosed information is authentic;
- the whistleblower undertakes action in good faith;
- the damage suffered as a result of the disclosure, if any, does not exceed the benefits accruing from the whistleblower's actions;
- sanctions against whistleblowers are proportionate.[294]

---

288 ECHR ruling of February 29, 2000, in Fuentes Bobo v. Spain, complaint No. 39293/98; ECHR ruling of July 16, 2009 in Wojtas Kaleta v. Poland, complaint No. 20436/02.

289 ECHR ruling of February 12, 2008 (The Grand Chamber) in Guja v. Moldova, complaint No. 14277/04.

290 ECHR ruling of July 21, 2011 in Heinisch v. Germany, complaint No. 28274/08.

291 Głowacka, Ploszka, Sczaniecki, *Wiem*, p. 13.

292 ECHR ruling of February 12, 2008 (The Grand Chamber) in Guja v. Moldova, complaint No. 14277/04.

293 Kondak, "Wolność," p. 49.

294 Głowacka, Ploszka, Sczaniecki, *Wiem*, p. 16.

When examining the above, the ECHR concluded that the authorities interfered with the freedom of expression.[295] Moreover, the interference was disproportionate and therefore infringed Article 10 of the Convention.[296] Since that ruling, the ECHR always examined the proportionality of state interference with the freedom expressed in Article 10 of the Convention through the prism of the above criteria.[297]

The ECHR applied these criteria also in e.g. Bucur and Toma v. Romania, which concerned the disclosure of wiretapping by the Romanian intelligence service.[298] In this case, the ECHR concluded that the public interest may outweigh the interests of the employer. The ECHR emphasized that although public officials were obliged to be more loyal and discreet towards the employer, they could also be covered by special protection e.g. against dismissal. In this case, the ECHR decided that the protection will be granted to the whistleblower, if the importance of the disclosed information for the public interest prevails over the obligation of secrecy towards the employer.

In Heinisch v. Germany,[299] the ECHR also extended protection to private sector employees who report irregularities.[300] This was another important ruling that affected the nature of the conventional protection of whistleblowers. The dispute concerned the dismissal of a nurse from a nursing home, following her notification to the prosecutor's office of a crime possibly committed by the employer. In its deliberations, the ECHR pointed to the obligation of the state to protect the freedom of expression, which also applies to relations governed by private law.[301] The ECHR's conclusion was that the criteria for granting protection to whistleblowers – mentioned

---

295 M. A. Nowicki, "Guja przeciwko Mołdawii – wyrok ETPC z dnia 12 lutego 2008 r., skarga nr 14277/04," in: *Europejski Trybunał Praw Człowieka. Wybór orzeczeń 2008*, ed. M. A. Nowicki, Wolters Kluwer Polska, Warszawa 2009, p. 214.

296 A. Ploszka, "Ochrona," p. 15.

297 Ploszka, "Ochrona," p. 15.

298 ECHR ruling of January 8, 2013 in Bucur and Toma v. Romania, complaint No. 40238/02.

299 ECHR ruling of July 21, 2011 in Heinisch v. Germany, complaint No. 28274/08.

300 Kondak, "Wolność," p. 55.

301 Ploszka, "Ochrona," p. 16.

above in the context of Guja v. Moldova – apply also to Heinish v. Germany. The ECHR considered that all of the criteria were met and underscored the fact that, among other things, the whistleblower first utilized the internal procedure for reporting irregularities and that she acted in good faith and in public interest.[302] The ECHR further held that public interest in being informed about the lack of institutional care provided to the elderly by a state-owned company is so important in a democratic society that it outweighs the interest in protecting the company's business reputation and interests.[303] In this case, the ECHR also found that the dismissal of the informant infringed Article 10 of the Convention. ECHR stated that the employer's failure to ensure an effective route for whistleblowers to report irregularities and for employers to respond appropriately justified the use of an external route for reporting irregularities. Although the ECHR case law does not explicitly say that the state must have provisions obligating it to provide legal protection to whistleblowers in the workplace, the above analysis clearly shows that – in certain circumstances – its absence may constitute a violation of the Convention.[304]

If we refer the above arguments to the activity of whistleblowers, we can conclude that their loyalty to the employer must not lead to them excluding the possibility of directing critical comments towards the employer.[305] The duty of loyalty is not absolute, and it is inferior to the public interest, should the seriousness and scale of the infringements be so important that it justifies the disclosure of such information by the employee.

Moreover, the ECHR examined the issue of whistleblowers' good faith. Here we must mention the grounds for the ruling in the case of

---

302 The ECHR held that care for the elderly, in particular when we consider the ageing of the population, was a matter of public interest.

303 Nowicki, *Europejski*, p. 391.

304 Ploszka, "Ochrona," p. 17.

305 Detailed argumentation of the Ombudsman on the dismissal of a Polish Radio journalist: Ombudsman of the Republic of Poland, "Szczegółowa argumentacja Rzecznika Praw Obywatelskich w sprawie zwolnionego dziennikarza Polskiego Radia," 2016, https://www.rpo.gov.pl/sites/default/files/Polskie%20radio%20-%20zwolniony%20dziennikarz.%20Argumenty%20RPO%20-%202.11.2016.pdf, access: 14.08.2019.

Marchenko v. Ukraine,[306] which contains a certain presumption of good faith in the activities of trade union representatives who reported observed irregularities.[307]

We must also note that the form of expression used by the whistleblowers will be important for granting protection to their activities. The ECHR in Palomo Sanches and Others v. Spain concluded that a statement made in a vulgar and degrading manner would not benefit from the protection the Convention provides.[308]

1.4 Whistleblower Protection in the Directive (EU) 2019/1937 of the European Parliament and of the Council of 23 October 2019 on the Protection of Persons Who Report Breaches of Union Law

On February 14, 2017, the European Commission was summoned by the Members of the European Parliament to urgently propose an "effective and comprehensive program for the protection of whistleblowers." In response, a draft version of the Directive, which included standards for the protection of whistleblowers,[309] was proposed by the European Commission in April 2018. Subsequently, on April 16, 2019, the European Parliament approved the Directive on the protection of persons who report on breaches of Union law[310] – the Whistleblower Protection Directive – accepted by the Council of the European Union on October 7, 2019; it was published in the Official

---

306 ECHR ruling of February 19, 2009 in Marchenko v. Ukraine, complaint No. 4063/04.

307 Ploszka, "Ochrona," p. 18.

308 See, in particular, the ECHR ruling of September 12, 2011, in Palomo Sanches and Others v. Spain, complaints No. 28955/06, 28957/06, 28959/06 and 28964/06.

309 Proposal for a Directive of the European Parliament and the Council on the protection of persons who report breaches of Union law (COM(2018) 218 final; 2018/0106 (COD); Whistleblower Protection Directive).

310 European Parliament legislative resolution of 16 April 2019 on the proposal for a directive of the European Parliament and of the Council on the protection of persons who report breaches of Union law (COM(2018)0218 – C8-0159/2018 – 2018/0106(COD)), http://www.europarl.europa.eu/doceo/document/TA-8-2019-0366_PL.html#title2, access: 18.08.2019.

Journal of the European Union on November 26, 2019.[311] The EU Member States are thus required to implement these provisions within two years.

The Whistleblower Protection Directive sets minimal guidelines for the Member States, while allowing them to refine details. They may also extend these provisions to other areas. It will be the first EU regulation to protect whistleblowers.[312] A study conducted by the European Commission in 2017,[313] which indicated the necessity for its introduction, estimates that – in the area of public procurement alone – the EU loses around €5.8–9.6 billion annually[314] due to the lack of sufficient protection for whistleblowers.

According to Article 1 of the Whistleblower Protection Directive, its objective is to improve the enforcement of EU law and policies by establishing standard guidelines, thus ensuring a high level of security for the persons who report breaches of Union law. Its regulations refer to the protection of whistleblowers who report on breaches EU financial interests and internal market rules, but also breaches in the following areas:

- public procurement;
- services, products, and financial markets, including the prevention of money laundering and financing of terrorism;
- product safety and their fulfillment of requirements;
- transport safety; environment protection;
- radiological protection and nuclear safety;
- food, fodder, health, and animal welfare safety;
- public health;
- consumer protection;
- privacy and personal data protection, and the security of networks and information systems.

---

311 https://eur-lex.europa.eu/legal-content/PL/TXT/?uri=CELEX:32019L1937.

312 G. Makowski, *Dyrektywa o ochronie sygnalistów przyjęta przez Parlament Europejski*, http://www.sygnalista.pl/dyrektywa-o-ochronie-sygnalistow-przyjeta-przez-parlament-europejski/, access: 28.08.2019.

313 L. Rossi, J. McGuinn, M. Fernandes, *Estimating the Economic Benefits of Whistleblower Protection in Public Procurement. Final Report – Study*, 2017, https://publications.europa.eu/pl/publication-detail/-/publication/8d5955bd-9378-11e7-b92d-01aa75ed71a1, access: 19.08.2019.

314 M. Gertig, "Dyrektywa w sprawie ochrony osób zgłaszających przypadki naruszenia prawa Unii," *Compliance* 2/2019, Instytut Compliance, p. 10.

Let us indicate that the above catalog does not include the sector of "employment, working conditions, workers' rights and the principle of equal opportunities, and equal treatment of men and women at work" proposed in the framework of the draft of the Whistleblower Protection Directive. The Member States may extend the scope of protection in their national legislation e.g. to areas not covered by this list. Noteworthy, according to recital 106 of, the transposition of the Whistleblower Protection Directive absolutely cannot reduce the level of protection already provided in the Member State to whistleblowers.

Article 4 of the Whistleblower Protection Directive broadly defines its subjective scope. Protection extends to the whistleblowers who work in both the public and private sector. A whistleblower, apart from an employee,[315] may also be a self-employed person, a stakeholder, a financial partner, a member of another company body, a volunteer, or a trainee, also one non-remunerated. Besides, anyone who works under the supervision and direction of contractors, subcontractors, and suppliers may be granted this status. The Directive also refers to persons whose employment relationship has already ended or is yet to be established; they can obtain certain information e.g. during admissions. According to Article 4(4) of the Act, protection will also apply, where appropriate, to persons who helped the whistleblower file the report, are linked to the whistleblower, and may thus experience retaliation – e.g. colleagues or relatives – and to individual legal entities e.g. owned by the whistleblower or otherwise linked to him.

Article 6 of the Whistleblower Protection Directive defines infringement as an unlawful act or omission, which refers to EU acts or their areas of application. It may also be contrary to the subject or purpose of EU regulations in the areas mentioned above. Furthermore, information about infringements means a fact or reasonable suspicion on actual or potential violations or attempts to conceal them, which occurred or are likely to occur in the organization in which the reporting person works, has worked, or has maintained contact in the context of their work. A whistleblower may raise a legitimate concern or suspicion and is not required to provide clear

315 I mean here employees according to Article 45 Paragraph 1 of the Treaty on the Functioning of the European Union, which also includes civil servants.

evidence.[316] On the other hand, recital 43 of the Whistleblower Protection Directive indicates that the spread of unjustified rumors or transfer of information fully accessible to the public will not benefit from the protection.

In order to report, the whistleblower has three procedural paths. One should first indicate the possibility of using an internal channel to transfer the information within a private or public legal entity. Recital 47 indicates that the whistleblower should be encouraged to use these channels and report infringements to their employer and reasonably expect that such a report will bring results.[317] However, the Whistleblower Protection Directive provides the possibility to skip this stage and make an external report, i.e. to relevant public agencies. The third path for whistleblowers is public disclosure, i.e. the release of information through the media.

The Whistleblower Protection Directive envisions that entities of the Member States – both in the private and public sectors – will be obliged to establish an internal channel and a reporting procedure for violations. Should national law so require, the procedure will occur after consultation and in cooperation with public stakeholders. Private entities with at least fifty employees are obliged to implement this procedure. However, the obligation may also be imposed by the Member States on entities with less than fifty employees. Thus, they require to conduct an appropriate risk assessment to consider the nature of their activities.[318] Furthermore, all public legal entities – including legal entities owned or controlled by public legal entities – are required to establish an internal channel and reporting procedure. However, one should highlight that a Member State may exempt from this obligation municipalities with less than 10,000 inhabitants or less than fifty employees or other entities with less than fifty employees.[319]

Article 9 of the Whistleblower Protection Directive sets procedures for internal reporting and follow-up actions. First, they must protect the

316 Gertig, "Dyrektywa," p. 11.

317 Gertig, "Dyrektywa," p. 11.

318 The Directive mentions in this context especially environmental and public health activities.

319 Noteworthy, the member states may make provisions for the establishment of internal notification channels common to several municipalities or operated by shared municipalities in accordance with national law, provided that they are separate and independent from the relevant external notification channels.

identity of the whistleblower and any third party mentioned in the report. Second, the person who submits the report should receive a confirmation of receipt within a maximum of seven days. One should also indicate that the entity (person or department) designated to follow-up actions must be impartial and act with due diligence. A reasonable time limit must also be set to provide feedback to the whistleblower of no longer than three months.[320]

According to recital 58 of the Whistleblower Protection Directive, the information provided to the whistleblower about the proceedings should be as comprehensive as possible, given the legal measures available.

Article 9 Paragraph 2 of the Whistleblower Protection Directive further specifies that internal channels must enable whistleblowers to submit a notification in writing, orally, via telephone, other voice communication systems, and in the form of a direct meeting (at the whistleblower's request). The Whistleblower Protection Directive leaves the decision whether to accept anonymous reports to the Member States.

In the case of reports through external channels, persons who report on breaches transfer information about irregularities directly to the appropriate agency or after the use of internal channels.[321]

Article 11 of the Whistleblower Protection Directive obligates the Member States to designate appropriate agencies to receive such reports, provide feedback, and follow-up actions upon notification. According to recital 65, these may be a judiciary agency, supervisory agency, or the Ombudsman.

Appropriate agencies will be required to establish independent channels to enable whistleblowers communicating malpractice in writing, orally, via telephone, via other voice communication systems, and during direct meetings (upon request).

External channels must be designed, established, and operated in a way that ensures the comprehensiveness, integrity, and confidentiality of information and to prevent unauthorized access by the staff of the appropriate

320 This deadline should be counted from the acknowledgment of receipt of the notification or, if no confirmation is received, from the expiry of the seven-day deadline after submitting the application.

321 Gertig, "Dyrektywa," p. 12.

agency.[322] Besides, it will be necessary to acknowledge the receipt of the report without delay; necessarily within seven days of receipt. Due diligence will be required in follow-up actions by the appropriate agency. However, information about undertaken actions will be transferred to the whistleblower within a reasonable period of time; not exceeding three months or, in justified cases, six months. Article 12 Paragraph 4 of the Whistleblower Protection Directive indicates that staff members of the agency will be designated and provided with specialized training to deal with external reports.

Furthermore, in compliance with Article 13 of the Whistleblower Protection Directive, the appropriate agencies will be required to publish on their websites information about the channels and procedures; i.e. the conditions of whistleblowers' eligibility for protection and the confidentiality rules about notifications.

Article 15 of the Whistleblower Protection Directive concerns public disclosures. A whistleblower benefits from protection in this procedure, if he first used internal and external channels (in some instances only the external), but their report was not processed within the prescribed time limit. A whistleblower may also use this route if they have reasonable grounds to believe that the breach may present an immediate or apparent threat to the public interest.[323] In the case of an external report, public disclosure is also possible if the whistleblower is at risk of retaliation or is unlikely to effectively prevent the breach due to particular circumstances, e.g. the risk of evidence destruction.

Chapter V of the Whistleblower Protection Directive, which deals with rules applicable to internal and external notifications, introduces the obligation for the Member States to ensure that the identity of whistleblowers – along with other information that enables their recognition – should not be disclosed without their expressed consent to anyone who is not an authorized member of staff competent to receive and follow up on reports. The disclosure of such information may take place only where it is a necessary and proportionate obligation under EU or national law in the context of federal investigations or judicial proceedings.[324]

322 Gertig, "Dyrektywa," p. 12.
323 For instance, in case of an emergency situation or risk of irreparable damage.
324 E.g. to guarantee the right to defense for the person mentioned in the notification.

Moreover, the Whistleblower Protection Directive applies to measures of security to whistleblowers. The most important one is the protection against any retaliation, direct or indirect, including threats and retaliation attempts; especially dismissal, suspension, salary reduction, degradation, discrimination, or mobbing. Article 20 of the Whistleblower Protection Directive requires the Member States to ensure that whistleblowers have access to support, which include free and open access to information and advice on procedures of legal protection, along with their rights.

Furthermore, the EU legislator decided that whoever undertakes activities damaging to the whistleblower is responsible for justifying the retaliatory actions; in court or during any other agency proceedings related to the person concerned. Regarding employment relationships, it will be the employer who will have the obligation to prove that the infringement report did not motivate the actions to aggravate the situation of the employee whistleblower.

Following Article 21 Paragraph 8 of the Whistleblower Protection Directive, the Member States must take necessary measures to provide a whistleblower – who follows a legal path of notification – all just remedies and full compensation for damages suffered. Persons who report on breaches of Union law must fulfill specific conditions to be protected. They should have reasonable grounds to believe the information is accurate at the time of notification; the report should be within the scope of the Whistleblower Protection Directive; they should make an internal, external, or public disclosure under the requirements of the Whistleblower Protection Directive.

The EU legislator offers the Member States the possibility to determine the penalties for the infringement on whistleblower protection; i.e. impeding whistleblower reporting, retaliation against whistleblowers, and breach of identity confidentiality. However, Article 23 Paragraph 1 of the Whistleblower Protection Directive indicates that the penalties are to be effective, proportionate, and deterring.

For the whistleblower protection system to work correctly, it must not be abused. One should use protection as intended in the Whistleblower Protection Directive. Therefore, the Member States must provide penalties and compensation measures also for persons who knowingly inform of or publicly disclose false notifications.

1.5 Summary

In an attempt to compare the above legal solutions, we should overview their most essential aspects in each country.

One should note that the USA has a highly developed and complex system of protection for whistleblowers. The False Claims Act and the Whistleblower Protection Act in the public sector are the most important provisions in this area, similarly to the Sarbanes-Oxley Act and the Dodd-Frank Act in the private sector. These are not the only American legal acts for the protection of whistleblowers.[325] The literature indicates that there are many state and federal US laws concerning reports on irregularities which, on the one hand, significantly differ[326] from one another and, on the other hand, often interact or overlap at state and federal levels.[327] The authors underline the fragmented approach to protecting whistleblowers by the creation of sectoral legislation.[328] For example, the False Claims Act refers only to reports of fraud against the government, while the Whistleblower Protection Act applies only to illegal activities within the federal administration. There is no single instrument that comprehensively covers all whistleblowers' actions throughout the country in both the public and private sector, regardless of the line of business.

The activity of US whistleblowers shows how much it can benefit the state. The US Department of Justice announcement from December 21, 2018,[329] further confirms it. It shows that, since 1986, when Congress

---

325 We may mention here also e.g. the Consumer Products and Safety Improvement Act of 2008, the Fraud Enforcement and Recovery Act of 2010, the Patient Protection and Affordable Care Act of 2010.

326 Dworkin, "US Whistleblowing," p. 36.

327 Henkel, "Whistleblower Rights."

328 Boyne, "Financial Incentives," p. 283.

329 U.S. Justice Department communique of December 21, 2018, is available at: U.S. Department of Justice, "Justice Department Recovers Over $2.8 Billion from False Claims Act Cases in Fiscal Year 2018," 2018, https://www.justice.gov/opa/pr/justice-department-recovers-over-28-billion-false-claims-act-cases-fiscal-year-2018. The 2018 False Claims Act statistics can be found at: U.S. Department of Justice, "Fraud Statistics – Overview," 2018, https://www.justice.gov/civil/page/file/1080696/download?utm_medium=email&utm_source=govdelivery, access: 19.08.2019.

significantly strengthened the provisions of the False Claims Act, more than $59 billion were recovered. In Fiscal Year 2018 alone, it was over $2.8 billion. The number of entries and the number of prizes awarded shows that the opportunity to receive a financial reward for their disclosure is an essential stimulus for whistleblowers to act. In this context, let us indicate that in the 2018 tax year alone, SEC received more than 5200 applications.[330] Besides, the Commission has awarded more than $168 million[331] in prizes to persons who report on breaches of US law[332] in this year. This amount reflects the importance of the information provided to the SEC by whistleblowers. The biggest prize ever awarded by the Commission was $49 million.[333] The opportunity to receive financial compensation for reporting violations triggered much discussion but, as the above statistics reveal, this has proven a sufficient incentive.[334] The literature argues that, for whistleblowers, the possibility of receiving a high price can be the most significant protection, because it enables them to cope with the loss of a job or slowdown in a career.[335]

The UK system of whistleblowers' protection is widely regarded in the literature as one of the best and most advanced in Europe.[336] The advantages of the discussed regulations include that they cover persons employed in both private and public sectors and offer a large number of available channels to report information. Whistleblowers may make protected disclosures to e.g. their employers, prescribed persons, or – in a broader context – the police or the media. Employees are encouraged to take internal actions first.

330 U.S. Securities and Exchange Commission, *2018 Annual Report to Congress: Whistleblowing Program*, 2018, p. 2, https://www.sec.gov/sec-2018-annual-report-whistleblower-program.pdf, access: 19.08.2019.

331 This amount exceeds the total amount allocated in all previous years.

332 U.S. Securities and Exchange Commission, *2018 Annual Report to Congress*, p. 1.

333 U.S. Securities and Exchange Commission, *Order Determining Whistleblower Award Claims*, March 19, 2018, https://www.sec.gov/rules/other/2018/34-82897.pdf, access: 24.08.2019.

334 Kutera, "Whisteblowing," p. 133.

335 Dworkin, "US whistleblowing," p. 44.

336 Kutera, "Whisteblowing," p. 138.; Waszak, "Związki zawodowe", p. 40; Wojciechowicz, "Sytuacja sygnalistów," p. 12.

However, after meeting certain conditions, they also benefit from protection by disclosing information outside the workplace. Persons dismissed or who suffered other damage due to their reports may file a complaint with the Employment Tribunal and – if deemed justified – receive compensation. Besides, whistleblowers who claim to the Employment Tribunal are required to demonstrate reasonable proof that their disclosure was made in public interest. It prevents the workers from using the protection granted to settle their private business.

The literature disagrees on the assessment of the abolishing of the requirement of "good faith" in protected disclosures. Nevertheless, this change allowed more people to report irregularities without fear of possible problems with their good intentions. However, we should remember that acting in bad faith may reduce the amount of compensation awarded by as much as 25 %.

Besides many undeniable advantages of the UK legislation, there also increase numbers of critical assessments, which indicating that after twenty years of practice the PIDA requires careful review, as it now offers less protection and places more burdens on whistleblowers than initially foreseen.[337] The report[338] prepared by the Thomson Reuters Foundation[339] and Blueprint for Free Speech[340] reviews case files and rulings of employment

---

337 M. Worth, S. Dreyfus, C. Lavite, G. Hanley, *Safe or Sorry: Whistleblower Protection Laws in Europe Deliver Mixed Results*, Blueprint for Free Speech, 2018, p. 17, https://www.changeofdirection.eu/assets/uploads/BLUEPRINT%20-%20Safe%20or%20Sorry%20-%20Whistleblower%20Protection%20Laws%20in%20Europe%20Deliver%20Mixed%20Results.pdf, access: 23.08.2019.

338 S. Wolfe, M. Worth, S. Dreyfus, *Protecting Whistleblowers in the UK: A New Blueprint*, 2016, https://blueprintforfreespeech.net/wp-content/uploads/2016/05/Report-Protecting-Whistleblowers-In-The-UK.pdf, access: 20.08.2019.

339 The Thomson Reuters Foundation stands for free, independent journalism, human rights, women's empowerment, and the rule of law, https://blueprintforfreespeech.net/wp-content/uploads/2016/05/Report-Protecting-Whistleblowers-In-The-UK.pdf, access: 20.08.2019.

340 Blueprint for Free Speech is a charity that provides research and analysis in support of freedom of expression for all people, as described in the UN Declaration of Human Rights. Blueprint For Free Speech, "About Us," https://blueprintforfreespeech.net/en/about/, access: 20.08.2019.

tribunal, media reports, research analyses, and studies, but also interviews with jurists, informants, experts, and lawyers. It concluded that the PIDA "is no longer capable of adequately protecting whistleblowers."[341] The main disadvantages of the regulation are the lack of protection of whistleblowers from retaliation, the cost and length of the system for reporting complaints to employment tribunals, and the lack of direct civil or criminal sanctions to deter, prevent, or discourage retaliation against whistleblowers.[342]

Romania is also considered to have some of the best legal solutions for the protection of whistleblowers.[343] However, the literature stresses that the execution of Romanian legislation in this area is lacking.[344] Furthermore, the lack of direct reference to the private sector should be considered a deficiency of this regulation.

On the other hand, according to Transparency International's report *Whistleblowing in Europe: Legal Protections for Whistleblowers in the EU* from 2013,[345] Slovenia is one of the countries with the highest level of protection for whistleblowers in the European Union.[346] Moreover, the OECD Working Group Bribery praised Slovenia for its legislation on the protection of whistleblowers and recommended raising awareness in the private sector and among state-owned companies about the protection provided.[347] Although some time has passed since these reports were published, Slovenia is still one of the countries with a high level of protection for whistleblowers. One can draw this conclusion in particular from the analysis of the provisions of its Integrity and Prevention of Corruption

341 S. Wolfe, M. Worth, S. Dreyfus, *Protecting Whistleblowers in the UK: A New Blueprint*, 2016, https://blueprintforfreespeech.net/wp-content/uploads/2016/05/Report-Protecting-Whistleblowers-In-The-UK.pdf, p. 3, access: 20.08.2019.

342 Worth, Dreyfus, Lavite, Hanley, "Safe or Sorry," p. 18.

343 Wojciechowicz, "Sytuacja sygnalistów," p. 13

344 Dimitriu, "Romania: First Steps," p. 259.

345 Worth, *Whistleblowing in Europe*, p. 8.

346 Besides Slovenia, the report remarks Luxembourg, Romania, and the UK.

347 OECD (2014e), *Phase 3 Report on Implementing the Anti-Bribery Convention in Slovenia*, www.oecd.org/daf/anti-bribery/SloveniaPhase3ReportEN.pdf, access: 28.08.2019, qtd. after OECD (2016), *Committing to Effective Whistleblower Protection*, OECD Publishing, Paris, p. 109.

Act of 2010, which provides for a wide range of internationally recognized good practices in the protection of whistleblowers.

The advantages of the above include the protection of whistleblower's identity and the protection from retaliation by employer. The support from the Commission for the Prevention of Corruption in the determination of a causal relationship between report and retaliation is essential. The bill does not contain a definition of such actions. Therefore, it is assumed that all activities in result of whistleblowers' reports that bring negative consequences on them, e.g. mobbing, will be regarded as retaliation. Another noteworthy procedure is the imposition of the burden of proof on the employer in the event of a dispute with a whistleblower, along with the possibility for government officials to be transferred to another equivalent position, should retaliatory measures against them ceased not, thus preventing further work on the current post. We should stress that the provisions of the bill protect only persons who act in good faith. However, a report in bad faith may result in several legal consequences for the whistleblower.

On the other hand, the literature argues that Integrity and Prevention of Corruption Act of 2010 lacks execution and that the Commission for the Prevention of Corruption is ineffective in its actions, even though it has a significant role in raising public awareness and solving problems related to the protection of whistleblowers.[348] Among the disadvantages of the Act is its broad scope that nevertheless only refers to cases of reports about potential corruption. Whereas regulations of the disclosure of illegal or unethical behavior concern only government officials. In other areas, only Slovenian Labor Code may apply, which does not provide for any special protection for whistleblowers, as in other countries.

Meanwhile, the Protected Disclosures Act in Irish law was a breakthrough in the protection of whistleblowers. The Protected Disclosures Act is one of the best in Europe. It is confirmed by the report *Best Practice Guide for Whistleblowing Legislation*,[349] published by Transparency International, which contains recommendations for the protection of whistleblowers. The Irish legislation is repeatedly cited as an example of a good or potentially

---

348 Peček, "Protection of Persons," p. 264.

349 *A Best Practice Guide for Whistleblowing Legislation*, Transparency International 2018.

good practice. Besides, in 2018, the Blueprint for Free Speech reported on the implementation of whistleblower legislation in the EU and gave the Irish legislation the highest rating among all the Member States in the protection of whistleblowers.[350]

The advantages of the Irish legislation include the coverage of employees in both the public and private sector, a wide range of channels for the disclosure of irregularities, and a broad scope of reportable infringements categories. The Act also provides high protection against retaliation by employers or third parties. If an employee is dismissed or otherwise punished or threatened with punishment as a result of their report, they may receive compensation of up to a maximum of five-years-worth of remuneration. Besides, the Act provides the right to take legal actions in respect of any damage suffered as a result of a protected disclosure. An exceptional procedure is also the possibility to reduce the amount of compensation due to the whistleblower's motivation.

As regards the regulation in Italy, the Law 179/2017 introduced a sound basis for the protection of whistleblowers. Among the advantages of its provisions, one should first highlight the introduction of a ban on retaliatory or discriminatory actions for reports on irregularities. Whereas, in case of a dispute, the burden of proof that the measures are unrelated to the notification is placed on the employer. Sanctions are provided for the violation of the above provisions. Moreover, one should emphasize the importance of the protection of whistleblowers' identity in the Law 179/2017, although without guarantees of anonymity in all court proceedings. However, the main disadvantage of the system is that it does not cover all the employees of the country. Not all actors in the private sector are obligated to adopt compliance programs under Decree 231. Therefore, they are not obligated to introduce whistleblower protection programs either. Therefore, there is a well-founded concern that – despite the introduction of high protection provisions – it will not cover whistleblowers in many private sector entities, especially in small and medium-sized enterprises, which have no links with public entities.

In France, the Sapin II Act guarantees a high level of protection for whistleblowers. The main advantages of the regulation are its broad

---

350 "Gaps in the System."

1. the Article 33 of the United Nations Convention against Corruption, ratified by Poland in 2006;[359]
2. the Article 9 of the Civil Law Convention of the Council of Europe on Corruption of November 4, 1999, ratified by Poland in 2002;[360]
3. the Council of Europe Parliamentary Assembly Resolution No. 1729 on the protection of whistleblowers of April 29, 2010,[361] and Resolution No. 2060 on increasing the protection of whistleblowers of June 23, 2015;[362]
4. the Recommendation of the Parliamentary Assembly of the Council of Europe No. 1916 of 2010;[363]
5. the Recommendation No. 7 of the Committee of Ministers of the Council of Europe on the protection of whistleblowers of April 30, 2014.[364]

However, the need to take action in this area among Polish authorities and institutions was recently stressed by e.g. the Ombudsman.[365] Moreover, also state authorities closely observe the matters of whistleblowers' activity,

---

359 *The United Nations Convention against Corruption*, adopted by the UN General Assembly on October 23, 2003. *Dziennik Ustaw* 84.563/2007.

360 *Dziennik Ustaw* 244.2443/2004.

361 Parliamentary Assembly of the Council of Europe, "Resolution 1729 (2010) Protection of whistle-blowers," 2010, http://assembly.coe.int/nw/xml/XRef/Xref-XML2HTML-en.asp?fileid=17851&lang=en, access: 18.08.2019.

362 Parliamentary Assembly of the Council of Europe, "Resolution 2060 (2015) Improving the protection of whistle-blowers," 2015, http://assembly.coe.int/nw/xml/XRef/Xref-XML2HTML-en.asp?fileid=21931&lang=en, access: 18.08.2019.

363 Parliamentary Assembly of the Council of Europe, "Recommendation 1916 (2010) Protection of whistle-blowers," 2010, http://assembly.coe.int/nw/xml/XRef/Xref-XML2HTML-EN.asp?fileid=17852&lang=EN, access: 18.08.2019.

364 Council of Europe, *Protection of Whistleblowers: Recommendation (CM/Rec(2014)7) Adopted by the Committee of Ministers of the Council of Europe on 30 April 2014 and Explanatory Memorandum*, 2014, https://rm.coe.int/16807096c7, access: 12.06.2019.

365 Ombudsman of the Republic of Poland, "The Ombudsman's letter to the Minister of Family, Labour, and Social Policy, of December 18, 2015, III.7040.104.2015 AF/LN," http://www.sygnalista.pl/wp-content/uploads/2016/10/List-RPO-MRPiPS-2015.pdf, access: 12.06.2019.

which is visible e.g. in the Draft Law on Transparency in Public Life scrutinized below or the Resolution No. 207 of the Council of Ministers of December 19, 2017, on the Government Anti-Corruption Program for 2018–2020.[366] This document considers the introduction of a unitary and coherent system of protection for whistleblowers a priority.

The 2018 PwC report *Who steals from Polish companies and how?* shows how important the activity of whistleblowers in Poland can be,[367] which is based on the eighth survey of economic crime; it reveals that whistleblowers helped detect as much as 45 % of all fraud in Polish companies.[368]

Finally, we should consider the 2019 report from a Poland-wide research *Gnębieni, podziwiani i… zasługujący na ochronę. Polacy o sygnalistach* (Oppressed, Admired, and… Deserving Protection: Poles on Whistleblowers).[369] The work provides impressive but unfortunately pessimistic conclusions about Poles' attachment to their workplace, the common good, and adherence to law.[370] The main objective of this project was to prepare and promote a Citizens' Draft Law, which would regulate the status of whistleblowers in Poland.[371] One of the questions asked during the survey concerned the respondent's attitude toward noticing a clear case of violation of law by a co-worker in the form of a bribe.

Only 26 % of respondents decided to inform their superiors about the situation. The number of people who declared that they would not do so was comparable, whereas as many as 29 % of respondents said that they did not know how they would behave in such a situation. It indicates that

---

366 Bill 207 of the Polish Council of Ministers of December 19, 2017 about the Govenrmental Program for Counteracting Corruption in 2018–2020.

367 PwC Polska, "Kto I jak okrada polskie firmy?" 2018, https://www.pwc.pl/pl/publikacje/2018/badanie-przestepczosci-gospodarczej-2018-raport-pwc.html, access: 12.09.2019.

368 For comparison, in 2016 the measurement reached only 9 %.

369 G. Makowski, M. Waszak, *Gnębieni, podziwiani i… zasługujący na ochronę. Polacy o sygnalistach. Raport z badania opinii publicznej*, 2018, p. 3, http://www.batory.org.pl/upload/files/Programy%20operacyjne/Forum%20Idei/Internet_Raport_sygnalisci_12-06.pdf, access: 22.08.2019.

370 M. Waszak, "Dlaczego nie cenimy sygnalistów?" 2019, http://www.batory.org.pl/blog_wpis/dlaczego-nie-cenimy-sygnalistow/, access: 12.09.2019.

371 Makowski, Waszak, *Gnębieni*, p. 3.

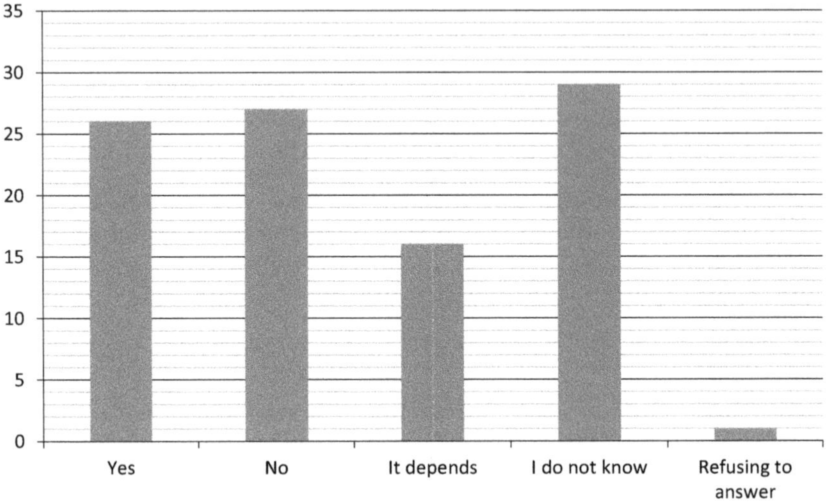

(Size N=1000)

Graph 1: Please imagine a situation where your work colleague accepts bribes in connection to his professional duties. Would you inform your superiors after discovering the fact?
Source: own elaboration based on G. Makowski, M. Waszak, *Gnębieni, podziwiani i... zasługujący na ochronę. Polacy o sygnalistach. Raport z badania opinii publicznej*, 2018, p. 12, http://www.batory.org.pl/upload/files/Programy%20operacyjne/Forum%20Idei/Internet_Raport_sygnalisci_12-06.pdf, access: 22.08.2019.

Poles have a problem with adopting an unambiguous attitude toward this type of issues.[372] The report also shows that the main demotivating factor for reporting irregularities is fear of being considered an informer and subjection to ostracism.[373] Poles' historical experiences strongly inform these choices. The many years of partitioning, German occupation during Second World War, and the period of communism afterwards contributed to a pejorative perception of any form of "denunciation." Whistleblowing is sometimes associated with cooperation with occupants' secret services or with

372 Makowski, Waszak, *Gnębieni*, p. 12.
373 Makowski, Waszak, *Gnębieni*, p. 2.

the security service and party apparatus of the Polish People's Republic.[374] As a result, the boundary between the notification of irregularities in good faith and public interest and ordinary denunciation is blurred.

Besides, in the absence of special protection for whistleblowers, fear of legal consequences repeatedly prevents Poles from acting. Whistleblowers are exposed to liability for e.g. infringement of personal rights (Article 24 of the Civil Code), defamation (Article 212 of the Civil Code), or disclosure of confidential information of the employer (Articles 265–267 of the Civil Code). In search of a model for the legal protection of whistleblowers in the workplace, we should analyze the provisions of the Polish Labor Code.

2.2 Whistleblower Protection in Polish Labor Law

2.2.1 The Law of June 26, 1974, in the Labor Code

The provisions of the Labor Code[375] do not directly regulate the notification of irregularities observed by employees as their duty or entitlement.[376] In this context, we should mention Article 100 Paragraph 2(4) of the Labor Code, which obligates employees to look after the good of the workplace and protect its property, but also to keep confidential all the information whose disclosure could expose the employer to damages. Employee's self-interest and the interest of the employee's team[377] determine the limits of this obligation. One should consider the good of the workplace as a common good of all members of the community.[378] An employee is obliged to fulfill this obligation in the interest of an employer or take necessary actions beyond the contractual conditions to reverse the financial or non-financial damage threatening the employer.[379]

374 Rogowski, "Whistleblowing," p. 23.

375 Act of June 26, 1974. Labor Code in *Dziennik Ustaw* 1040/2019.

376 Raczkowski, *Ekspertyza w sprawie ochrony osób zatrudnionych sygnalizujących nieprawidłowości przed nadużyciami ze strony podmiotu zatrudniającego*, Kielce 2009, p. 2.

377 Wujczyk, "Podstawy whistleblowingu," p. 116.

378 For more, see Bolesta, "Sygnalizacja," p. 41.

379 A. Kosut, "Dbałość o dobro zakładu pracy jako źródło obowiązku lojalności pracownika wobec pracodawcy," *Annales UMCS – sectio G (Ius)* 65.2/2018, Wydawnictwo Uniwersytetu Marii Curie-Skłodowskiej, Lublin, p. 112.

In this context, one should discuss the position taken by the Supreme Court in its decree of October 1, 1998,[380] which states that an employee is obligated to inform the employer about risks to the good of the workplace and to inform the employer about any knowledge of actions to the employer's detriment. Failure to comply may be considered a severe violation of essential employee obligations. Such notification is undoubtedly a fulfillment of the duty of loyalty towards the employer. The work regulations or the employment contract also specify this obligation. One should also underline another Supreme Court decree,[381] which states that the above violation of the obligation will be an indiscriminate accomplishment of an unlawful order which, at least potentially, threatens the interests of the employer, while its harmfulness is known to the employee. One should also highlight the jurisprudence of the European Court of Human Rights (ECHR), which shows that the scope of the duty of loyalty toward the employer is not the same in every profession. Less loyalty is required of e.g. journalists. Their right and duty is to comment on matters of public importance; these include the organization of work or the functioning of the media, which realize the public mission.[382] On the other hand, service in uniformed formations like the army or the police is linked with severe discipline, an obligation of loyalty to superiors, and preservation of the integrity of the workplace.[383] Particular loyalty must also be shown by e.g. civil servants.[384] However, we should emphasize that this does not completely deprive them of their right to criticism. The ECHR ruling of July 21, 2011,[385] declares that the employee's duty of loyalty toward the employer is in some cases subordinated to the right to public disclosure of information on infringements at work. Here, the conflict between the duty of loyalty and the employer contradicts the possibility of public disclosure

380 Supreme Court ruling of October 1, 1998, I PKN 351/98.
381 Supreme Court ruling of June 2, 2010, II PK 364/09.
382 ETHR ruling of February 29, 2000, in Fuentes Bobo v. Spain, No. 39293/98; ETHR ruling of July 16, 2009, in Wojtas-Kaleta v. Polsce, No. 20436/02.
383 Głowacka, Ploszka, Sczaniecki, *Wiem*, p. 23.
384 ETHR ruling of February 2, 2008, in Guja v. Moldova, No. 14277/04.
385 ETHR ruling of July 21, 2011, in Heinisch v. Germany, No. 28274/08, qtd. after M. A. Nowicki, *Europejski Trybunał Praw Człowieka. Wybór orzeczeń 2011*, Wolters Kluwer Polska, Warszawa 2012, p. 391.

of irregularities. Moreover, the ECHR mentions the right to permitted criticism and protection against negative consequences for notification of irregularities in several other cases,[386] some of which will be described below.

Polish jurisprudence also confirms these views and conclusions. An employee has the right to permitted public criticism of the superior – the right for whistleblowing – when it does not lead to violation of his obligations, which primarily consist of care for the good of the workplace and nondisclosure of information, which could expose the employer to harm – the duty of loyalty – along with adherence to the company's rules of social coexistence.[387] The literature describes employer criticism as an obligation for the sake of the good of the workplace.[388] Criticism is permitted if it is consistent with the legal order,[389] it is formulated in an appropriate form and place, and it is justified.[390] The above allows us to deduce the employee's legitimacy to disclose irregularities at work.[391]

In search of the sources of no explicit regulation of employee obligation of whistleblowing, we should quote the content of Article 100 Paragraph 2(6) of the Labor Code, according to which an employee is especially obligated to observe the principles of social coexistence in the workplace. The legislator did not specify which behavior is considered compatible with or contrary to the principles of social coexistence. However, the literature indicates that the provision of Article 100 Paragraph 2(6) of the Labor

---

386 ETHR ruling of November 25, 1997, in Grigoriades v. Greece, No. 24348/94; ETHR ruling of May 20, 1999, in Rekvenyi v. Hungary, No. 24348/94. See also ETHR ruling of January 8, 2013, Bucur and Toma v. Romania, No. 40238/02, described in Chapter III.

387 Supreme Court ruling of August 28, 2013, No. I PK 48/13.

388 A. Nowak, "Wygaśnięcie stosunku pracy na skutek wykluczenia ze spółdzielni pracy a ochrona członków związków zawodowych. Glosa do wyroku Sądu Najwyższego z dnia 16 czerwca 2005 r., I PK 257/04," *Gdańskie Studia Prawnicze – Przegląd Orzecznictwa* 4.16/2006, Wydawnictwo Uniwersytetu Gdańskiego, Gdańsk, p. 169.

389 Supreme Court ruling of October 13, 1999, No. I PKN 269/99, OSNP 4.114/2001.

390 A. Drozd, "Dopuszczalna krytyka pracodawcy (przełożonych) w orzecznictwie Sądu Najwyższego," *Praca i Zabezpieczenie Społeczne* 8.25/2012, Polskie Wydawnictwo Ekonomiczne, Warszawa, pp. 23–26.

391 Cf. Bolesta, "Sygnalizacja," p. 41; Raczkowski, *Ekspertyza*, p. 14.

Code imposes on employees the obligation to comply with the principles of social coexistence currently required in the Polish society, along with the standards of conduct accepted by the company, regardless of whether they directly or indirectly relate to the organization of work.[392] Jurisprudence found that what disagrees with the principles of social coexistence is e.g. the giving of false evidence regarding facts commonly known to the crew in proceedings after an accident.[393] Therefore, we should state that the duty of compliance includes the obligation to apply non-legal norms, in particular moral, manners-related, social, ethical, and customary norms; in a word, the general and specific rules in a given workplace.[394] Behavior contrary to the principles of social coexistence may be the basis for a penalty or even termination of contract.

Therefore, we should recognize that the disclosure of behaviors that violate the principles of social coexistence in the workplace would implement the obligation to comply with these principles.

Measures to protect whistleblowers against retaliatory actions for the disclosure of irregularities can be found primarily in the provisions concerning the employer's obligation to counteract discrimination in employment, i.e. Articles 18^{3a}–18^{3e} of the Labor Code. Noteworthy, Article 32 Paragraph 2 of the Constitution of Poland,[395] states that no one may be discriminated in political, social, or economic life for any reason. Whereas, in accordance with Article 18^{3a} Paragraph 1 of the Labor Code, employees should be treated equally in the establishment and termination of employment relationship, conditions of employment, promotion and access to training for the improvement of professional qualifications, regardless of gender, age, disability, race, religion, nationality, political opinion, trade

---

392 A. M. Świątkowski, "Article 100." In: *Kodeks pracy. Komentarz.* Wydawnictwo C. H. Beck, Warszawa, 2018, https://sip.legalis.pl/document-view.seam?documentId=mjxw62zogi3damrqgy3denjoobqxalrugi4tinbxguza, access: 11.09.2019.

393 Supreme Court ruling of January 12, 1998, No. I PKN 458/97.

394 K. Ziółkowska, "Obowiązek przestrzegania zasad współżycia społecznego w relacji do pracowniczego obowiązku dbałości o dobro zakładu pracy," *Studia Prawnoustrojowe* 28/2015, Wydawnictwo Uniwersytetu Warmińsko-Mazurskiego, Olsztyn, p. 242.

395 Constitution of Poland of April 2, 1997. *Dziennik Ustaw* 78.483/1997.

union membership, ethnic origin, religion, sexual orientation, employment for a fixed or indefinite period, and full-time or part-time employment. According to Article 18^{3d} of the Labor Code, a person toward whom the employer breached the principle of equal treatment has the right to compensation in the amount not lower than the minimum wage. Moreover, Article 18^{3e} Paragraph 1 of the Labor Code states that an employee's exercise of rights from the breach of the principle of equal treatment in employment cannot be the basis for the unfavorable treatment of the employee, and it cannot cause any negative consequences for the employee, especially constitute a cause for the termination of the employment relationship or its termination without notice.

Moreover, the above protection also applies to the employee who supported another employee in exercising the rights from the principle of equal treatment in employment from Article 18^{3e} Paragraph 2 of the Labor Code. The notion of granting support used in the provision in question is of broad significance. Such support may be an attempt to counteract discrimination against a whistleblower by intervening with the employer or by witnessing in court proceedings in the case of a discriminated employee.[396] It is a typical activity of whistleblowers.[397]

Moreover, according to Article 94^3 Paragraph 1 of the Labor Code, the employer is obligated to counteract mobbing. Mobbing means actions or behaviours concerning an employee or directed against an employee, consisting in persistent long-term harassment or intimidation of the employee, causing the employee's underestimation of own professionalism, causing or aimed at humiliating or ridiculing the employee, isolating them or eliminating their colleagues from the team (Article 94^3 Paragraph 2 of the Labor Code). According to Article 94^3 Paragraph 3 of the Labor Code, if harassment caused an employee's ill health, the employee may claim an appropriate amount from the employer as financial compensation for the harm suffered. Besides, an employee who was subject to mobbing or terminated work relationship due to mobbing has the right to claim compensation from the employer in the amount not lower than the minimum

396 L. Florek, T. Zieliński, "Art. 18(3(e))," in: *Kodeks pracy. Komentarz*, ed. L. Florek, ed. VII, Wolters Kluwer Polska, Warszawa, 2017, pp. 172–173.

397 Wujczyk, "Podstawy whistleblowingu," p. 119.

and inform the social labor inspector about it. Apart from the above rights, the company social inspector is entitled to issue written recommendations to the employer in the form of recommendations to manage the identified infringements within a specified time (Article 11 of the Law on Social Labor Inspection). We may conclude that there is an obligation to signalize irregularities detected in the workplace.

Let us notice that social labor inspectors are obliged by law to cooperate with the National Labor Inspectorate and other supervisory and control bodies (Article 17 Paragraph 1 of the Law on Social Labor Inspection), to which they may report observed irregularities. The National Labor Inspectorate should provide social assistance to the labor inspector in the performance of their tasks, in particular through legal counseling, specialist press, and training.[428]

Moreover, the employment relationship of a social labor inspector shall be subject to special protection against dismissal during the term of office and within one year after its expiry, unless there are reasons that justify the termination of the employment contract without notice (Article 13 Paragraph 1 of the Law on Social Labor Inspection). In such a case, the termination of the employment contract may occur after obtaining prior consent of the statutorily competent authority of the trade union. Even if the employee is guilty of serious misconduct, the courts should take into account the employee's right to protection,[429] which ensures that social labor inspectors are protected in their independence and performance of duties.

2.2.4 The Law of April 13, 2007, on the National Labor Inspectorate

We should also refer to the regulations concerning the activities of the National Labor Inspectorate. It is a body appointed to supervise and control the observance of labor law, especially the regulations and principles of health and safety at work. It also regulates the legality of employment within the scope specified in the Law on the National Labor Inspectorate.[430]

---

428 T. Liszcz, *Prawo pracy*, Wolters Kluwer Polska, Warszawa 2019, p. 589.
429 The Supreme Court judgment of May 8, 2014, III PK 110/13.
430 Article 1 of the Law of April 13, 2007, on the National Labor Inspectorate, *Dziennik Ustaw* 1251/2019.

At the request of employees or their representatives concerning health and safety, labor inspectors of the National Labor Inspectorate conduct inspections and apply legal measures provided for in the provisions of the National Labor Inspectorate.[431] In the reply to parliamentary question 8304 on the legal protection of whistleblowers,[432] the Secretary of State at the Ministry of Labor and Social Policy stated on October 1, 2012,[433] that,

> In case of doubts of employees concerning the compliance of employer's conduct with the Law on the National Labor Inspectorate, it is possible to request assistance, including a request for intervention, from the locally competent regional labor inspectorate. The Labor Inspectorate is equipped with appropriate powers and means to perform tasks related to supervision and control, along with the enforcement of employers' compliance with the current legislation. Pursuant to Article 23(2) of the Law on the National Labor Inspectorate,[434] if there is a justified concern that an employee's disclosure of information to a labor inspector in matters covered by the inspection could expose that employee to any damage or accusation due to the provision of this information, the labor inspector may issue a decision to keep secret the circumstances that would disclose the identity of the employee, including their personal data.

We may conclude that the labor inspector has the right to keep whistleblower's identity secret if there is a concern of negative consequences for the employee due to the disclosure of certain information. Moreover, according to Article 44 Paragraph 3 of the Law on the National Labor Inspectorate, its controllers are obliged to not disclose information that the control is conducted as a result of a complaint unless the complainant consents to it in writing. The guarantee of an employee's anonymity based on the mentioned provisions may undoubtedly encourage the reporting of irregularities.

---

431 Wojciechowska-Nowak, "Skuteczna ochrona prawna sygnalistów," p. 9.

432 Parliamentary Question No. 8304 of August 29, 2012, to the Minister of Labor and Social Policy on the legal protection of "whistleblowers," http://www.sejm.gov.pl/sejm7.nsf/InterpelacjaTresc.xsp?key=01A1F464, access: 12.12.2018.

433 Response of the Secretary of State in the Ministry of Labor and Social Policy of October 1, 2012, to the Parliamentary Question No. 8304 on the legal protection of "whistleblowers," http://www.sejm.gov.pl/sejm7.nsf/InterpelacjaTresc.xsp?key=543A7299, access: 12.12.2018.

434 Concerns the Law of April 13, 2007, on the National Labor Inspectorate, *Dziennik Ustaw* 1251/2019.

Moreover, the Law on Macroprudential Supervision introduced new regulations to Article 83a of the Law on Trading in Financial Instruments.[441] According to Article 83a Paragraph 1a, the investment firm is required to have procedures for anonymous reports of the violations of law to the indicated board member and – in exceptional cases – to the supervisory board, including Regulation 596/2014,[442] Regulation 600/2014,[443] and the ethical procedures and standards in force in the investment company. However, Article 83a Paragraph 1b of the Law states that – within the procedures referred to in Paragraph 1a – the investment firm protects employees who report violations at least against activities of a repressive nature, discrimination, and other types of unfair treatment. The last provision introduced is Article 83a Paragraph 1c, under which – in the case of a brokerage house operating as a partnership – the requirements referred to in Paragraph 1a apply to general partners who have the right to conduct cases of the company or represent it pursuant to the provisions of the Law of September 15, 2000 on the Commercial Companies Code.

Detailed guidelines for anonymous reports referred to in Article 83a Paragraph 1a of the Law on Trading in Financial Instruments are currently determined in Chapter 4 (Paragraph 32) of the Regulation of the Minister of Finance of May 29, 2018, on detailed technical and organizational conditions for investment firms and banks referred to in Article 70 Paragraph 2 of the Law on Trading in Financial Instruments and Trust Banks.[444] Paragraph 32 of the Law contains requirements for anonymous

441 The Law of July 29, 2005, on Trading in Financial Instruments, *Dziennik Ustaw* 2286/2018.

442 EU Regulation No. 596/2014 of the European Parliament and of the Council of 16 April 2014 on market abuse (market abuse regulation) and repealing Directive 2003/6/EC of the European Parliament and of the Council and Commission Directives 2003/124/EC, 2003/125/EC and 2004/72/EC.

443 EU Regulation No. 600/2014 of the European Parliament and of the Council of 15 May 2014 on markets in financial instruments and amending Regulation (EU) No 648/2012.

444 The Regulation of the Minister of Finance of May 29, 2018, on detailed technical and organizational conditions for investment companies and banks referred to in Article 70 Paragraph 2 of the Law on Trading in Financial Instruments and Trust Banks, *Dziennik Ustaw* 1111/2018. It replaced the Regulation of the Minister of Development and Finance of April 25, 2017, on

reports, which are practically identical to the ones presented above in the Regulation of the Minister of Development and Finance on the internal control system in banks.

Some argue that the above provisions were the first to introduce the legal regulation of protection strictly related to whistleblowers.[445] Let us indicate that the adoption of these regulations was part of the implementation of Article 71 of the so-called CRD IV Directive (Capital Requirements Regulation 2013),[446] which imposes on EU member states the obligation to establish effective and reliable mechanisms for the notification of competent authorities of potential or actual infringements of national provisions in the area regulated by this Directive and EU Regulation of the European Parliament and the Council of EU No. 575/2013.[447]

2.3.2 The Law of July 29, 2005, on Capital Market Supervision; the Law of May 27, 2004, on Investment Funds and Alternative Investment Fund Management; and the Law of June 9, 2011, on Geological and Mining Law

Among the laws that impose the obligation of procedures for anonymous notification of regulations on certain entities also include the Law of July 29, 2005, on Capital Market Supervision,[448] the Law of May 27, 2004,

---

detailed technical and organizational conditions for investment companies and banks referred to in Article 70 Paragraph 2 of the Law on Trading in Financial Instruments and Trust Banks, *Dziennik Ustaw* 855/2017.

445 Hryniewicz, Krak, *Sygnaliści*, p. 14.

446 EU Directive No. 2013/36/EU of the European Parliament and of the Council of 26 June 2013 on access to the activity of credit institutions and the prudential supervision of credit institutions and investment firms, amending Directive 2002/87/EC and repealing Directives 2006/48/EC and 2006/49/EC.

447 EU Regulation No. 575/2013 of the European Parliament and of the Council of 26 June 2013 on prudential requirements for credit institutions and investment firms and amending Regulation (EU) No 648/2012, in: Hryniewicz, Krak, *Sygnaliści*, p. 14.

448 The Law of July 29, 2005, on Capital Market Supervision, *Dziennik Ustaw* 1417/2018.

Investment Funds and Alternative Investment Fund Management,[449] and the Law of June 9, 2011, on Geological and Mining Law.[450]

According to Article 3b of the Law on Capital Market Supervision, entities such as investment firms' agents, trust banks, companies operating a regulated market, or companies operating commodity exchanges are required to have procedures for the anonymous reports of violations of EU Regulation 596/2014,[451] committed by their employees to a designated member of the management board and, in individual cases, to the supervisory board. Based on the delegation in Article 3a Paragraph 3 of the Law on Capital Market Supervision, the Minister of Finance issued the Regulation of June 25, 2018, on the reception of reports on violations of EU Regulation 596/2014 by the Polish Financial Supervision Authority.[452] Its provisions determine the possibility of notification via electronic devices, in writing, by phone, or in person.

In turn, Article 237b of the Law on Investment Funds and Alternative Investment Fund Management imposes on entities like investment fund companies or fund management companies the obligation to implement procedures for the anonymous reporting of violations committed by employees of these entities of its provisions to a designated member of the management board and – in exceptional cases – to the supervisory board; in the absence of such bodies: to a designated general partner or partner authorized to conduct company cases following the provisions of the Code of Commercial Companies.

The Geological and Mining Law is another legal act which implements EU regulations on reporting irregularities.[453] It concerns Directive 2013/30/EU of the European Parliament and of the Council of EU of June 12, 2013, on the safety of oil and gas activities in maritime areas along with the

449 The Law of May 27, 2004, on Investment Funds and Alternative Investment Fund Management, *Dziennik Ustaw* 1355/2018.

450 The Law of June 9, 2011, on Geological and Mining Law, *Dziennik Ustaw* 868/2019.

451 EU Regulation No. 596/2014.

452 Regulation of the Minister of Finance of June 25, 2018 on the reception by the Polish Financial Supervision Authority of reports of violations of EU Regulation 596/2014, *Dziennik Ustaw* 1262/2018.

453 Hryniewicz, Krak, *Sygnaliści*, p. 23.

amendment of the Directive 2004/35/WE of the European Parliament and the Council of EU.[454] Under Article 117c of the Geological and Mining Law, in the case of exploration, identification, or extraction of hydrocarbons from deposits within the maritime areas of the Republic of Poland, the Mining Operations Unit Head shall locate information – in a generally accessible place within the premises of the mining plant – about the possibility of the anonymous reporting of safety and environmental problems related to such activities to the competent authority and the President of the State Mining Authority of the Republic of Poland. Moreover, the Mining Operations Unit Head shall inform the persons present within the premises of the mining plant about such a possibility, especially during each training course in the field of health and safety at work. Moreover, the President of the State Mining Authority is obliged to publish a telephone number in the Public Information Bulletin on the website of the relevant office, through which the above problems should be reported. While reporting the problems, it is not necessary to provide data enabling the identification of the applicant. The analysis of the applications itself is also conducted anonymously. Noteworthy, a Mining Operations Unit Head who did not display information about the above possibility of anonymous reporting of problems or did not inform persons present on the premises of the mining plant about this possibility, especially during each training course in the field of health and safety at work, may be fined.

2.3.3 The Law of April 16, 1993, on Combating Unfair Competition

On September 4, 2018, the provisions of the Law of July 5, 2018, amending the Law on Combating Unfair Competition and certain other acts[455] of importance for whistleblowers entered into force. This act introduced significant amendments to the Law of April 16, 1993, on Combating Unfair

454 EU Directive 2013/30/EU of the European Parliament and of the Council of 12 June 2013 on safety of offshore oil and gas operations and amending Directive 2004/35/EC.

455 The Law of July 5, 2018, Amending the Law on Combating Unfair Competition and Certain Other Laws, *Dziennik Ustaw* 1637/2018.

1, obliged institutions must develop and implement an internal procedure for the anonymous reporting by employees or other persons performing activities for the obliged institution of actual or potential violations of anti-money laundering and anti-terrorism financing regulations. Hence, the channel enabling reports of irregularities should be available not only to employees of obliged institutions but also to other persons who perform activities for the benefit of the institution. A broad catalog of addressees of the above obligation is contained in Article 2 Paragraph 1 of the Law. The catalog includes domestic banks, branch offices of foreign banks, branch offices of credit institutions, cooperative savings and credit unions, the National Cooperative Savings and Credit Union, domestic payment institutions, domestic electronic money institutions, investment firms, trust banks, foreign legal persons conducting brokerage activities in the territory of the Republic of Poland, companies operating a regulated market – to the extent that they operate an auction platform – investment funds, alternative investment companies, investment fund companies, entrepreneurs conducting currency exchange activities, notaries within the scope of activities performed in the form of a notarial deed, attorneys, legal advisors, foreign lawyers, tax advisors within the scope of providing legal assistance, or tax advisory services to the client within the scope in question.

Pursuant to Article 53 Paragraph 2 of the Law on Counteracting Money Laundering and Terrorism Financing, the procedure of anonymous reporting of infringements of provisions on counteracting money laundering and terrorism financing specifies:

1) a person responsible for receiving notifications;
2) the manner of receiving reports;
3) how to protect the employee that issues the report, ensuring at least protection against repressive actions, discrimination, and other types of unfair treatment;
4) how to protect personal data of the reporting employee and the person alleged to have committed a breach, following the provisions on the protection of personal data;
5) the rules of confidentiality in the case of disclosure of the identity of persons referred to in point 4, or when their identity can be established;

6) the type and nature of follow-up actions taken after the reception of the notification;
7) the deadline for the removal of personal data contained in the notifications by obliged institutions.

The provisions of the Law also provide for administrative penalties for failure in the implementation of internal procedures for anonymous reporting.[465] According to Article 150 of the Law on Counteracting Money Laundering and Terrorism Financing, these penalties include:

a) the publication of information about the obliged institution and the scope of violation of the provisions of the Law by this institution in the Public Information Bulletin on the website of the office of the minister in charge of public finance;
b) the order to cease particular actions by the obliged institution;
c) the withdrawal of concession or permit or deletion from the register of a regulated activity;
d) the ban on performing managerial duties by a person responsible for the breach of the provisions of the Law by an obliged institution for a period not exceeding one year;
e) financial penalty.

The Law provides for two instances of notification: it is possible to transfer information about detected irregularities to the management board, but also to the General Inspector of Financial Information as a governmental body.[466]

In the performance of the delegation under Article 80 Paragraph 3 of the Law on Counteracting Money Laundering and Terrorism Financing, the Minister of Finance issued the Regulation of May 16, 2018, on Receiving Notifications of Infringements of Provisions on Counteracting Money Laundering and Financing of Terrorism.[467] It defines how the General Inspector for Financial Information collects reports of actual or potential

465 Jasiński, "Sygnalizacja o nieprawidłowościach," p. 15.
466 Jasiński, "Sygnalizacja o nieprawidłowościach," p. 15.
467 Regulation of the Minister of Finance of May 16, 2018, on Receiving Notifications of Infringements of Provisions on Counteracting Money Laundering and Financing of Terrorism, *Dziennik Ustaw* 959/2018.

violations of provisions on anti-money laundering and financing of terrorism. The General Inspector for Financial Information may collect the reports from employees, former employees of obliged institutions, or other persons who perform or performed activities for the benefit of obliged institutions on the basis other than an employment relationship, may also define how reports are handled and stored, and how the information on actions allowed after the report is accepted.[468]

The provisions of the Regulation on the reception of notifications impose on the General Inspector for Financial Information the obligation to create the possibility of receiving notifications in electronic version and paper form. However, these are not anonymous notifications, as the person who reports is obliged to indicate the means of contact in the notification: an e-mail address or a correspondence address. The General Inspector for Financial Information may ask the notifying person for explanations regarding the information provided. The means of communication adopted by the General Inspector for Financial Information are:

a) independent of the means of communication used in the ordinary course of activities of the General Inspector;
b) ensuring the confidentiality, integrity, and availability of the information, including its protection against unauthorized reading;
c) allowing for the storage of notifications in a manner ensuring a follow-up by the General Inspector.

The lack of the possibility of an anonymous signaling activity in the Regulation may have an impact on the number of whistleblowers who dare to provide information necessary for the General Inspector for Financial Information. The literature stresses that this approach is incomprehensible in the context of the provisions of the Law on Counteracting Money Laundering and Terrorism Financing, which provides for such a procedure.[469] Moreover, the above regulations narrow down the list of violations that can be reported by whistleblowers only to those in the

468 Paragraph 1 of the Regulation of the Minister of Finance of May 16, 2018, on Receiving Notifications of Infringements of Provisions on Counteracting Money Laundering and Financing of Terrorism, *Dziennik Ustaw* 959/2018.

469 Hryniewicz, Krak, *Sygnaliści*, p. 23.

field of counteracting money laundering and terrorism financing, which does not give them the possibility to disclose other types of irregularities. Nevertheless, let us indicate that these provisions constitute another essential step in the Polish legislation in the area of the system of reports of irregularities by whistleblowers.

2.3.5 The Law of June 6, 1997, on the Code of Criminal Procedure and the Law of June 6, 1997, on the Penal Code

We should also discuss the criminal law provisions that may apply in practice to whistleblower activities.[470] Under criminal law, both in material and formal terms, there are no provisions directly relating to the protection of whistleblowers. The expressions such as "the injured party" or "the witness" cannot be considered synonymous with the concept of the whistleblower. Nevertheless, we should mention Article 304 of the Code of Criminal Procedure,[471] which concerns reports on irregularities and provides for a social obligation to report suspicions of a crime. According to Paragraph 1 of this provision, everyone who knows of an offense prosecuted ex officio has the social obligation to notify the prosecutor or the Police. This obligation is not subject to any legal liability in the event of its abandonment. It is only an expression of a moral obligation incumbent on citizens.[472] Exceptions to this rule are crimes listed in Article 240 of the Penal Code.[473] They include genocide, espionage, murder, or seizure of a ship or aircraft. A person who has credible information about a punishable preparation, attempt, or committing a prohibited act listed in the Law and who does not immediately notify an authority appointed to prosecute crimes shall be subject to the penalty of deprivation of liberty for up to three years.

In the context of this social obligation to report suspicions of a crime, there is doubt whether these provisions do not give rise to abuse by persons

470 For more, see Szymczykiewicz, *Miejsce,* pp. 396–401.

471 The Law of June 6, 1997, of the Code of Criminal Procedure, *Dziennik Ustaw* 1987/2018.

472 Derlacz-Wawrowska, "Whistleblowing," p. 396.

473 The Law of June 6, 1997, of the Penal Code, *Dziennik Ustaw* 1600/2018.

in this respect shall be conducted without the participation of the parties and shall be kept "secret" or "top secret." Anonymized information about the witness is available for the court and prosecutor only; if necessary also for the police officer conducting the proceedings. The provisions do not contain a catalog of prohibited acts in cases of the application of witness protection. Therefore, we should recognize that the status of anonymous witness may be obtained in the case of any crime.[483] Since the above regulation guarantees anonymity to the person who gives testimony – including whistleblowers – it may also be an excellent incentive for whistleblowers to undertake signaling activities in their places of employment.

2.4 Summary

To summarize, there is no legal act in the Polish law that comprehensively regulates the legal situation of whistleblowers. The legal concept of whistleblower status, signaling activities, and legal protection for whistleblowers has not yet been developed. Moreover, I believe that the current legislation does not create an effective legal framework for the protection of whistleblowers. The regulations in this area are scattered in various acts and are not consistent with one another. The literature indicates that the legal protection of whistleblowers in Poland has two basic shortcomings: a narrow scope and low effectiveness of available legal instruments in court proceedings.[484]

We should note that employees have a duty of signaling activity at the workplace. When taking any actions, the whistleblower should bear in mind the obligation to consider the employer's reputation. However, this obligation is not absolute. We should emphasize that the lack of appropriate regulations and – consequently – the lack of protection for whistleblowers discourage employees to disclose information about detected irregularities. As practice shows, employees are thus exposed to negative consequences, such as discrimination, mobbing, or dismissal, which can sometimes be difficult to challenge in court. This is mainly due to difficulties with evidence

483 T. Grzegorczyk, *Kodeks postępowania karnego*, Vol. 1, Articles 1–467, Wolters Kluwer Polska, Warszawa 2014, p. 638.

484 Wojciechowska-Nowak, "Skuteczna ochrona prawna sygnalistów," p. 20.

in proceedings before the labor court, mainly in terms of demonstrating by whistleblowers that the reason indicated in the notice is merely apparent. The literature indicates that the employee's argumentation about reported irregularities is irrelevant in court proceedings, as the subject of examination is the reason for the termination of the employment relationship indicated by the employer, e.g. liquidation of the workplace.[485] Moreover, even granting compensation to an employee or restoring them to work after long court proceedings can rarely be considered adequate to the moral, health, or material losses incurred. Noteworthy, in the case of employment on the basis of a temporary employment contract, when terminating the contract with an employee, the employer does not have to give any reason, so the court does not examine the legitimacy of termination. Whereas persons employed under civil law contracts are, in fact, beyond any protection whatsoever.

We should take notice of the emergence of the first provisions relating to the activities of whistleblowers in the Polish legal system. Let us emphasize that the above occurred as part of the implementation of EU regulations. A similar case is pending in connection with the adoption of the directive on the protection of individuals who report infringements of the EU law, whose regulations are discussed in this publication.

Moreover, we witness a noticeable increase in the interest in whistleblowers' activities among employers themselves, who increasingly often create internal procedures that enable employees to report irregularities. They can be an effective tool to warn against abuses in the organization. We should indicate that these systems often differ from one other. The most complex of them includes both the creation of documents, e.g. ethical codes, and solutions that facilitate reporting irregularities, e.g. the establishment of special anonymous hotlines or ethics officers.[486] The literature highlights that a number of guaranteed information paths is important for the correct functioning of such procedures.[487] In practice, the following channels of reporting irregularities are used:

485 Wojciechowska-Nowak, "Skuteczna ochrona prawna sygnalistów," p. 18.
486 Waszak, *Sygnaliści*, p. 137.
487 Waszak, *Sygnaliści*, p. 137.

a) in person, through contact with a member of the management or a specially designated person, such as an Ethics Officer;
b) via e-mail to an address specifically designated for this purpose;
c) via phone: to a special number, sometimes free of charge;
d) via the Internet: by means of an anonymous data encryption form;
e) via an external professional legal person e.g. a law firm.

The key to the success of these procedures is the awareness of potential whistleblowers of their existence and functioning. It is necessary to train employees in the use of signaling paths and explain the importance of these activities for the good of the company. Moreover, the employer's attitude towards compliance with the proposed procedures is important. If in practice they prove ineffective or give no anonymity despite assurances, employees will lose interest in them and will not want to share information.[488] It seems necessary to provide at least one way of anonymous reporting of abuse. It enables action to be taken without fear of negative consequences e.g. dismissal. On the other hand, open reports should ensure the protection of whistleblowers' identities and comply with the provisions on personal data protection. Thanks to this, the employee will not be afraid of ostracism or retaliation from other employees on behalf of their superiors.[489] Some employers also allow outside parties, such as business partners, to use internal reporting systems. Therefore, not only an employee but also a customer or contractor can become a whistleblower in such procedures.[490]

---

488 P. Chmiel, "T-MOBILE POLSKA," in: *Systemy zgłaszania nieprawidłowości, Założenia do ustawy o ochronie sygnalistów*, Global Compact Network Poland, Warszawa, 2018, p. 30, https://ungc.org.pl/wp-content/uploads/2018/09/Za%C5%82o%C5%BCenia-do-ustawy-o-oschronie-sygnalist%C3%B3w.pdf, access: 16.08.2019.

489 A. Wojciechowska-Nowak, *Założenia do ustawy o ochronie osób sygnalizujących nieprawidłowości w środowisku zawodowym. Jak polski ustawodawca może czerpać z doświadczeń państw obcych?*, Fundacja im. Stefana Batorego, Warszawa, 2012, p. 20.

490 I. Czerwińska-Engel, "3M POLAND," in: *Systemy zgłaszania nieprawidłowości, Założenia do ustawy o ochronie sygnalistów*, Global Compact Network Poland, Warszawa, 2018, p. 26, https://ungc.org.pl/wp-content/uploads/2018/09/Za%C5%82o%C5%BCenia-do-ustawy-o-oschronie-sygnalist%C3%B3w.pdf, access: 16.08.2019.

Anti-discrimination and anti-mobbing policies deserve special attention among all the procedures introduced for reporting embezzlement[491]. These help employers to meet their obligations to counteract discrimination and mobbing in workplaces and to prevent these negative phenomena. These undoubtedly make it easier for employees to conduct signaling activities.

However, these reporting procedures do not necessarily enjoy the trust of employees and do not always meet the standards of actual protection. Company whistleblowers face e.g. cultural barriers.[492] Moreover, employers are reluctant to consult internal regulations with employees or their representatives, which results in a lack of agreement and mutual trust between the social partners. Despite the above, the implementation of in-company procedures that enable employees reporting irregularities should be considered good practice, which brings measurable benefits to the employers themselves. Moreover, the application of such procedures helps to promote the idea of whistleblowing in the Polish employee circles.[493]

491 Wujczyk, "Podstawy whistleblowingu," p. 118.
492 Wojciechowska-Nowak, "Skuteczna ochrona prawna sygnalistów," p. 3.
493 Wujczyk, "Podstawy whistleblowingu," p. 119.

Chapter III Proposal of Whistleblower's Legal Protection Model in the Workplace in Poland

3.1 Preliminary Remarks

We should also discuss the legal regulations proposed at the time of the preparation of this study, which more or less relate to the reporting of irregularities and protection of whistleblowers, i.e. the Draft Law on Transparency in Public Life and the Draft Law on the Liability of Collective Entities for Criminal Offences. Their introduction into the Polish legal order may remedy the lack of an effective legal framework for the protection of whistleblowers in Poland. As I will present below, these regulations provide a number of valuable legal instruments for the protection of whistleblowers. Moreover, we should pay special attention to the Citizens' Draft Law on Whistleblowers' Protection, which contains many solutions I support. Besides the above regulations, this chapter will also present a doctrine proposal for a model of legal protection of whistleblowers at work.

3.2 Draft Laws

3.2.1 Draft Law on Transparency in Public Life

One of the regulations mentioned in the Preliminary Remarks to this chapter is the Draft Law on Transparency in Public Life.[494] From the very beginning, the Draft Law was subject to many reservations and comments from both private and public legal persons,[495] including the Polish Ombudsman.[496] In 2018, works on the Draft Law ceased with no communication about the

494 The website of the Government Legislation Center since January 8, 2018, offers the latest version of the Draft Law on Transparency in Public Life: https://legislacja.rcl.gov.pl/projekt/12304351.

495 Wojciechowicz, "Sytuacja sygnalistów," p. 13.

496 Ombudsman of the Republic of Poland, "Opinion of the Ombudsman on the Draft Law on Transparency in Public Life, of January 22, 2018," https://www.rpo.gov.pl/pl/content/opinia-rpo-w-sprawie-projektu-ustawy-o-jawnosci-zycia-publicznego, access: 23.10.2018.

Polish government's withdrawal from work on the planned legal act.[497] According to the definition proposed in Article 2 Paragraph 1(15) of the Draft Law, the definition of a whistleblower is a natural person or entrepreneur whose cooperation with the judiciary consists in reporting information about the possibility of committing a crime by an legal person with which they are bound by an employment contract, business relationship, or other contractual relationship that may adversely affect the informant's professional, material, or life situation and for which the prosecutor grants the status of whistleblower. The list of offences covered by this regulation appears in Article 61 of the Draft Law and includes bribery, paid protection, participation in an organized group or criminal association, or fraud. Hence, the whistleblower cooperates with the judicial system and receives such a status from the prosecutor who assesses e.g. the reliability of the submitted information.[498] The status of the whistleblower may also be granted at the request of the police authorities or the President of the Supreme Audit Office. Once a decision on the aforementioned subject is issued, the whistleblower would receive special protection against potential retaliatory actions.[499] In accordance with Article 63 Paragraph 1(1) of the Draft Law, in employer-employee relations such protection includes e.g. prohibition on the termination of an employment contract or an employment relationship with a whistleblower or on changing the terms of an employment contract or an employment relationship to a less favorable one.[500] If – as a result of submitting information – the employment relationship or official relationship is terminated without the consent of the prosecutor, the whistleblower will be entitled to compensation in the amount of twice the annual salary collected on the last position held. Moreover, the whistleblower may be granted reimbursement of legal representation costs. The proposed regulations stipulate that the protection of whistleblowers is to continue for a period of one year after the conclusion of proceedings.[501]

---

497 Hryniewicz, Krak, *Sygnaliści*, p. 32.
498 Hryniewicz, Krak, *Sygnaliści*, p. 32.
499 Jasiński, "Sygnalizacja o nieprawidłowościach," p. 15.
500 For more, see Bolesta, "Sygnalizacja," p. 35–46.
501 From the date of discontinuation of proceedings or termination by a final ruling of criminal proceedings instituted against the perpetrator of the crime.

Moreover, the possibility of awarding interest to the person who received whistleblower status or to an enterprise run by that person, if the offender has been convicted as a result of a reported crime.

According to Article 68 Paragraph 1 of the Draft Law, an entrepreneur who owns at least a medium-sized enterprise as defined in the Act of July 2, 2004, on the freedom of economic activity[502] must apply internal anti-corruption procedures to prevent cases of specific crimes committed by persons who act in the name or on behalf of that entrepreneur. Moreover, Article 68 Paragraph 2 binds directors of the public finance sector units to develop and apply internal anti-corruption procedures in subordinate units to prevent cases of the commitment of above crimes. Noteworthy, the above regulations do not ensure the anonymity of whistleblowers.

The Draft Law envisages severe consequences for the violation of its regulations. These include fines of up to PLN 10,000,000 for e.g. failure to develop internal anti-corruption procedures, failure to apply such procedures, or their apparent or ineffective character.[503]

3.2.2 Draft Law on the Liability of Collective Entities for Criminal Offences

Another proposed regulation relevant to this study is the Draft Law on the Liability of Collective Entities for Criminal Acts.[504] The Law is already in force in the Polish legal system since 2002. However, due to its ineffectiveness, the legislature began work to modify the previously introduced regulations.[505] The Draft Law specifies e.g. the obligation for collective legal persons to accept notifications of irregularities, mandatory internal procedures to clarify the notification, and specific measures to protect whistleblowers in the event of retaliatory actions by collective legal persons.[506]

502 Law of July 2, 2004, on the freedom of economic activity, *Dziennik Ustaw* 2168/2017. The Law expired due to the entry into force of the Law of March 6, 2018, the Entrepreneurs' Law, *Dziennik Ustaw* 1292/2019.

503 Hryniewicz, Krak, *Sygnaliści*, p. 33.

504 http://orka.sejm.gov.pl/Druki8ka.nsf/Projekty/8-020-1211-2019/$file/8-020-1211-2019.pdf.

505 Hryniewicz, Krak, *Sygnaliści*, p. 33.

506 Jasiński, "Sygnalizacja o nieprawidłowościach," p. 16.

Reference to whistleblowers already appears in Article 1 Paragraph 1(3), which states that the Draft Law specifies the rules of liability of collective legal persons related to actions against persons who report irregularities. Detailed regulations on this subject appear in Chapter 4 "The Liability of Collective Entities in Relation to Actions Against Whistleblowers." A collective legal person is considered a legal legal person and an organizational unit without a legal status, whose separate provisions grant legal capacity, including a commercial company with the State Treasury shareholding, a local government unit, or a union of such units, a limited liability company in an organization, a liquidated legal person, and an entrepreneur who is not a natural person, excluding the State Treasury, local government units, and their unions.

According to the Draft Law regulations, the whistleblower may be an employee of a collective legal person, a member of a body, or a person acting on its behalf or in its interest on the basis of a legal act. According to Article 11 Paragraph 1 of the Draft Law, the authorities of the collective legal person and in particular the designated body of the collective legal person supervising compliance with the rules and regulations governing the activity of the legal person or persons exercising internal supervision (collective legal person authorities) shall take steps – within the scope of their power – to clarify the information reported by the whistleblower. The whistleblower may report:

1) the suspicion of the preparation, attempt, or execution of a prohibited act;
2) the breach of duties or misuse of powers by the authorities of the collective legal person or certain persons who act in its name or on its behalf;
3) the failure to exercise due diligence required under the circumstances by the collective legal person's authorities or certain persons who act in its name or on its behalf;
4) irregularities in the organization of activities of a collective legal person which could lead to a criminal offence.

Upon receiving information on irregularities, collective legal person authorities should conduct an investigation, in which they verify the information and establish the circumstances of the case. If they fail to comply with this obligation or remove the irregularities or infringements identified in the course of the investigation that facilitated or enabled the commission of the offence, the court may hold the collective legal person liable for the offence and impose a fine of up to PLN 60,000,000.[507] Noteworthy, the regulations in question do not mention anything about ensuring anonymity or even confidentiality for individuals who report the information. The regulations merely provide, in Article 11 Paragraph 3 of the Draft Law, that the collective legal person authorities should endeavor to ensure that employees who report the information are protected at least from any repressive action, discrimination, or otherwise unfair treatment. It is doubtful whether this desire to provide protection against potential retaliation will be sufficiently encouraging for whistleblowers to report irregularities.

Further proposed regulations stipulate that, if the employee's rights have been infringed or the employment relationship or mutual agreement with the whistleblower has been terminated as a result of the disclosure of information, the court may decide at the whistleblower's request:

1) to reinstate them;
2) to compensate them for damage;
   - should the information reported be relevant and allowed for the prevention of the offence or allowed for its swifter detection.

This does not apply if the whistleblower was the perpetrator of a criminal offence related to the activities of the collective legal person, unless the whistleblower disclosed all the relevant circumstances of the offence to the collective legal person and the law enforcement authority. Thus, whistleblowers will be entitled to a claim for reinstatement or compensation, if their information is found relevant and helpful and if, in principle, they are not the perpetrator of the criminal act in question. Article 13 Paragraph 3 of the Draft Law states that – when ruling on compensation for breach of employee rights or termination of employment agreement – the court determines its amount in a manner specified in the provisions of the

507 In accordance with Article 17 Paragraph 1 of the Draft Law, there is a financial penalty of PLN 30,000–30,000,000. However, in the discussed situation, Article 12 Paragraph 1 stipulates that the court, recognizing a collective entity as responsible for the criminal act, may impose a fine up to twice the upper limit.

- the guarantee of data confidentiality, including the protection of whistleblower's identity and personal data of the persons concerned;
- the specification of the mode of reporting;
- the assurance of whistleblower's protection against retaliation;
- the assurance of a reliable and objective verification of the reported information.

The Citizens' Draft Law provides for mandatory consultation of the above procedures with trade unions. This will enable shaping them with the participation of interested parties, who may identify problems that have not been noticed by the employing legal person. Let us indicate that public finance legal persons are required to create internal procedures for whistleblowing.

Article 9 of the Citizens' Draft Law guarantees the protection of the identity of the whistleblower. The disclosure of whistleblower's data is possible only with the consent of the informant or – under certain circumstances – with the consent of the court.

The proposed regulations prohibit taking or threatening to take any retaliatory action against a whistleblower, including but not limited to discrimination, dissolution of the legal relationship between the whistleblower and the employer, or changing working conditions to less favorable. In the event of the deterioration of the whistleblower's situation as a result of the signaling action, such a person is entitled to compensation from the employer in the amount proportional to the degree of such deterioration, not less than PLN 10,000. Moreover, a whistleblower may demand reinstatement to work under the previous conditions or compensation equal to the last remuneration received for the period of two years. The burden of proof that the deterioration of the whistleblower's position is not retaliation for signaling action would lie with the employer. If the whistleblower bears the costs of legal representation in cases concerning the abovementioned protection, they are entitled to reimbursement of these costs by the employer.

Furthermore, Article 10 Paragraph 2 of the Citizens' Draft Law stipulates that any retaliatory measures against the person who reports irregularities within three years from the date of becoming aware of them by the employer are null and void by virtue of law. The proposed regulations also provide for the exclusion of whistleblowers from legal liability for the violation of legally protected secrecy and personal rights and provide for access to free legal assistance.

In accordance with Article 15 Paragraph 1 of the Citizens' Draft Law, a Commission for the Protection of Whistleblowers is to be established to monitor compliance with the Law, which would consist of the Ombudsman, representatives of the government, employees, employers, and non-governmental organizations. The Commission's term of office would be six years, and its tasks would include: collecting information on notifications of irregularities received by competent authorities, monitoring their management, and issuing opinions on draft normative acts concerning the activity of whistleblowers or dissemination of protection standards in this area.

The Citizens' Draft Law also envisages a fine or a non-custodial sentence in the event of retaliation against a whistleblower that would lead to serious or irreparable damage to his health or an underestimation of his professional competence. However, the following activities are punishable by fine alone:

- disclosure of information allowing to establish the identity of the whistleblower in a manner contrary to the Act;
- failure to introduce an internal procedure for reporting irregularities in the public finance sector unit in accordance with the law or failure in its application;[512]
- deliberate report of false information by the whistleblower.

3.3 Doctrinal Proposal

The following subchapter will propose legal solutions for the protection of whistleblowers that could be applied in the Polish legal system. I believe that the best solution would be to regulate this matter in a separate Act of law that will comprehensively set the legal framework for the activities of whistleblowers and the scope and prerequisites for granting them protection. The proposed assumptions of the regulation are as follows:

1. The law should cover both the public and private sectors.

512 In this case, the head of a public finance sector unit would be subject to a fine.

2. The scope of the Act should be determined by the definition of the whistleblower. This status could apply to any natural person that discloses irregularities or information justifying the suspicion of irregularities, but also a person that provides any assistance in these activities. In this context, the nature of the legal relationship between the whistleblower and the legal person to which the reported irregularities relate is irrelevant. In particular, protection should be available regardless of the form of employment, so that its scope would cover not only employees within the provisions of the Labor Code but also, among others, officials in an employment relationship, the self-employed, volunteers, and those employed under civil law contracts or providing services to a given legal person on another basis. Moreover, this status should also be available to applicants for employment and persons who already ceased cooperation with the legal person concerned by the application e.g. after termination or expiration of the employment relationship. Protection should also apply to certain legal legal persons, such as those owned by or otherwise associated with a whistleblower.
3. The reported irregularities or information that justifies the suspicion of their occurrence may concern an action or omission that will be inconsistent with the provisions of generally applicable law or will otherwise threaten the public interest. Examples of irregularities include: the creation of a threat to public security, the violation of public and legal obligations, including taxes, and the violation of human rights or corruption.
4. Several reporting paths must be established. Moreover, we the chronology of their use is equally important. As a first step, irregularities should be disclosed internally, i.e. within a public or private body, e.g. an employer or a designated person. The whistleblower should also be able to omit this stage and inform directly the public authority competent to receive such information, then report back, and follow up the reports. Such an authority may be e.g. a judicial, a supervisory body, or the Ombudsman. Only after the ineffective use of at least one of the above paths or when their use is impossible or clearly inappropriate for legitimate reasons, should it be permissible to disclose the information to the public, e.g. to the media. A good reason sample clause applies e.g. when the whistleblower has reasonable grounds to believe

that the reported infringement may present a direct or obvious threat to the public interest, e.g. in the event of an emergency or a risk of irreparable harm.

5. All public and private sector bodies with at least fifty employees should be required to establish internal systems for signaling irregularities. Other legal persons should do this on a voluntary basis. Such systems should be established in agreement with trade unions that operate on the employer's premises, so that the demands of employees can be taken into account, i.e. the demands of those directly concerned by the proper functioning of such procedures. Moreover, these procedures should meet certain standards, e.g.:
   a) identify the proper person or organizational unit to follow up on the notification;
   b) enable a notification to be made in writing, orally, or by any other means of communication, e.g. online;
   c) ensure the confidentiality of whistleblower's identity and that of the implicated legal person;
   d) guarantee a fair verification of reported information within a reasonable period of time and take appropriate measures should infringements be confirmed;
6. The Act should specify the prerequisites for granting protection to whistleblowers. In my opinion, they should entail:
   a) acting in good faith, i.e. having reasonable belief that the information provided is true, even if it is not confirmed in reality;
   b) acting in public interest, i.e. activities motivated by revenge or aimed at personal or financial gain should be excluded from protection;
   c) reporting via routes and in accordance with the rules established in the Act.
7. Legislation should provide for a legal presumption that signaling activities were undertaken in good faith. We should repeat here the premises for the rebuttal of the presumption from the Citizens' Draft Law on Whistleblowers' Protection.[513] Namely, such rebuttal is possible when:

513 http://www.sygnalista.pl/projekt-ustawy/.

above, there is no doubt that the Draft Law would constitute an important step in the development of legal standards in the field of whistleblowing. In particular the granting of special protection to whistleblowers against potential retaliatory measures and the obligation for certain legal persons to apply internal anti-corruption procedures to prevent crimes committed by individuals who act in the name of or on behalf of a whistleblower should be viewed positively.

In reference to the Draft Law on the Liability of Collective Entities for Criminal Offenses, we should indicate that it pays much attention to the protection of individuals who report irregularities. The proposed regulations concern not only combating prohibited activities but also preventing them, which may protect collective legal persons from negative consequences in the future. The above should be assessed positively in the context of whistleblowing. However, one flaw here is the failure to ensure the anonymity and confidentiality of whistleblowers. This may prevent the proper functioning of systems for signalizing irregularities in collective legal persons.[519]

In turn, should the above-described Citizens' Draft Law on Whistleblowers' Protection come into force, it would be the first comprehensive source of protection for whistleblowers in Poland. The vast majority of the proposed solutions deserve our approval. Above all, it is only right to provide protection for natural persons who report information in good faith and in public interest, which they acquired in connection with their duties, work, or contract. Therefore, the protection would extend to persons who have a many legal relationships with the subject of the notification. Such a solution would enable not only employees but also persons who obtained information by other means to benefit from the protection. Undoubtedly, this procedure increases the chances of detecting and disclosing more irregularities. A positive aspect in this context is also the extension of protection to those who assist in the reporting of an irregularity by another person. An unquestionable advantage of the project is also the broad definition of the types of irregularities that may be reported. Moreover, we should emphasize that the Citizens' Draft Law allows reporting to three different types

519 Hryniewicz, Krak, *Sygnaliści*, p. 34.

of recipients and indicating the chronology of their choice, with priority given to the use of the internal path.

As for possible feedback on the Citizens' Draft Law, we should consider extending the protection to those involved in the pre-employment process who may become aware of irregularities in the course of such activities. I believe that a positive step would also be to obligate the implementation of the system of reporting irregularities not only for public finance sector legal persons but also for private sector legal persons, which employ e.g. at least fifty people.

Moreover, this chapter proposes a doctrinal model of legal protection for persons who communicate irregularities in the workplace to persons or entities capable of taking effective action to stop these practices.

The presented measures are intended to enable whistleblowers to act without fear of negative consequences. The measures result from the analysis of literature, case law, and selected legal acts in the field of protection of whistleblowers, conducted by this study. The proposed legal solutions take into account the assumptions of the EU directive on the protection of whistleblowers approved in 2019. Moreover, the measures mostly coincide with proposals presented in the Citizen's Draft Law on Whistleblowers' Protection prepared by the Stefan Batory Foundation, the Helsinki Foundation for Human Rights, the Forum of Trade Unions, and the Institute of Public Affairs.

Conclusion

The studies cited in this book show that the activity of whistleblowers is one of the most effective instruments for detecting irregularities in the workplace. Moreover, the introduction and smooth functioning of internal reporting procedures is an indispensable element of effective risk management in an organization. The activity of whistleblowers is sometimes the only chance to detect undesirable phenomena. Reporting irregularities at an early stage may prevent the occurrence of damage or reduce its extent.

However, signaling activities still raise doubts as to their interpretation, and those who decide to do so face numerous difficulties. This publication highlights a number of problems in the protection of whistleblowers in Polish labor law, such as the narrow scope of protection and the ineffectiveness of existing legal instruments available in the course of court proceedings. As a result, there is no effective protection of whistleblowers in the current legal status. Moreover, employees in Poland who notice irregularities in the workplace often do not know how to behave in such a situation and where to seek support. Moreover, we should also indicate that existing legal regulations do not meet the requirements resulting from international recommendations.[520]

Therefore, the activity of whistleblowers in Poland is burdened with personal risk. As practice shows, such people are exposed to negative consequences of their actions, such as discrimination, mobbing, or termination of employment, which cannot be easily challenged in court. This is mainly due to evidential difficulties, especially in terms of demonstrating by whistleblowers that the reason for their dismissal is apparent or that the irregularities they uncovered find confirmation in reality. The above does not encourage employees to undertake signaling action.

There is no possibility to improve the situation of whistleblowers in Poland without the introduction of appropriate legal regulations. Hence,

---

520 Recommendation CM/ Rec(2014)7 Protection of whistleblowers, Rada Europy, Strasburg, April 30, 2014, http://www.coe.int/t/DGHL/STANDARDSETTING/CDcj/CDCJ%20Recommendations/CMRec%282014%297E.pdf, access: 12.02.2019.

this book proposes a model of protection for such persons, which aims at filling this gap in the Polish legal order. This is the result of an analysis of the literature, case law, and selected legal acts from around the world in the field of whistleblower protection.

The aim of the solutions presented in Chapter III was to create real support and protection for persons who report on irregularities in the workplace. This goal is to be achieved by, among other things:

- including in the definition of a whistleblower the largest possible group of people; not only current and former employees but also candidates for employment and persons who provide assistance in whistleblowing activities; regardless of the nature of the legal relationship between the whistleblower and the entity to which the reported irregularities relate, in particular regardless of the basis of employment;
- protecting the people employed in both public and private sectors;
- creating several channels for reporting irregularities and indicating the chronology of their use; in an internal forum or directly to the competent public authority and, in cases specified by law, disclosure to the public;
- imposing an obligation on certain entities to implement internal whistleblowing systems;
- conditioning the protection of whistleblowers on the fulfilment of certain premises, such as acting in good faith, in the public interest, and in accordance with procedures delineated in the legislation;
- a number of protective measures: the presumption of good faith in actions of whistleblowers, the confidentiality of their data, the possibility of anonymous reporting, the prohibition of retaliation, or the transfer of the burden of proof that actions against a whistleblower were not retaliatory to the entity that undertook them.

The Polish legislator will have to take action in this respect due to the obligation to implement the provisions of the EU Directive, discussed in the earlier part of the book. However, the implementation of the Directive's provisions may encounter certain adaptation difficulties, which result from the unprecedented nature of the proposed solutions in the Polish legal system. Other barriers may include negative stereotypes that function in the Polish society in the perception of whistleblowers as informers and the failure to notice the potential of whistleblowing about perceived irregularities. Hence, apart from legislative work, of great importance will be activities aimed at raising public awareness of the very essence of the whistleblowing phenomenon.

Bibliography

Andrzejewski, Marek. "Whistleblowing, czyli demaskacja pracownicza w zarządzaniu zasobami ludzkimi." *Acta Universitatis Lodziensis. Folia Oeconomica* 288/2013, Wydawnictwo Uniwersytetu Łódzkiego, Łódź, pp. 275–286.

Arszułowicz, Marek. "Whistleblowing, czyli ujawnianie w dobrej wierze." *Prakseologia* 147/2007, Instytut Filozofii i Socjologii Polskiej Akademii Nauk / Akademia Leona Koźmińskiego, Warszawa, pp. 91–113.

Association of Certified Fraud Examiners. "Report to the Nations: 2018 Global Study on Occupational Fraud and Abuse." 2018. https://www.acfe.com/report-to-the-nations/2018 (12.04.2019).

Becker's Hospital Review. "11 Things to Know About the False Claims Act," 2010, https://www.beckershospitalreview.com/news-analysis/eleven-things-to-know-about-the-false-claims-act.html (19.08.2019).

Blueprint For Free Speech. "About Us," https://blueprintforfreespeech.net/en/about/ (20.08.2019).

Blueprint for Free Speech. "United Kingdom – Whistleblowing Protection." 2014. https://blueprintforfreespeech.net/document/united-kingdom (13.07.2019).

Blueprint for Free Speech. "Gaps in the System: Whistleblower Laws in the EU." 2018. https://www.changeofdirection.eu/assets/uploads/BLUEPRINT%20-%20Gaps%20in%20the%20System%20-%20Whistleblowers%20Laws%20in%20the%20EU.pdf (26.08.2019).

Bolesta, Łukasz. "Sygnalizacja jako przejaw obowiązku lojalności wobec pracodawcy?", *Annales UMCS – sectio G (Ius)* 65.2/2018, Wydawnictwo Uniwersytetu Marii Curie-Skłodowskiej, Lublin, pp. 35–46.

Bolesta, Łukasz. "Ujawnianie nadużyć przez sygnalistów a ochrona tajemnicy przedsiębiorstwa." In: *Prawne, ekonomiczne i finansowe uwarunkowania rozwoju przedsiębiorstw*, eds. Paweł Antonowicz, Paweł Galiński, Paulina Nogal-Meger, Wydawnictwo Uniwersytetu Gdańskiego, Gdańsk, 2019, pp. 125–136.

Bondarenko, Peter. "Enron scandal." 2016. https://www.britannica.com/event/Enron-scandal (14.05.2019).

Bowie, Norman E. and Ronald F. Duska. *Business Ethics*. Prentice Hall, Englewood Cliffs New Jersey, 1990.

Boyne, Shawn M. "Financial Incentives and Truth-Telling: The Growth of Whistle-Blowing Legislation in the United States." In: *Whistleblowing: A Comparative Study, Ius Comparatum – Global Studies in Comparative Law 16*, eds. Gregor Thusing, Gerrit Forst, Springer International Publishing, Cham, 2016, pp. 279–310.

Burczyc, Agnieszka. "Ustawa Sarbanesa-Oxleya i jej następstwa dla działalności audytorów oraz zarządów spółek." *Prace Naukowe Uniwersytetu Ekonomicznego we Wrocławiu* 268/2012, Wydawnictwo Uniwersytetu Ekonomicznego we Wrocławiu, Wrocław, pp. 43–53.

Centralne Biuro Antykorupcyjne. "Program nagradzania demaskatorów," http://www.antykorupcja.gov.pl/ak/czy-wiesz-ze/9129,Program-nagradzania-demaskatorow.html (12.07.2019).

Chmiel, Piotr. "Sygnalizowanie nieprawidłowości (whistleblowing)." *Przegląd Antykorupcyjny* 7/2016, Wydawnictwo Centrum Szkolenia Policji w Legionowie, Warszawa, pp. 41–43.

Chmiel, Piotr. "T-MOBILE POLSKA." In: *Systemy zgłaszania nieprawidłowości, Założenia do ustawy o ochronie sygnalistów*, Global Compact Network Poland, Warszawa, 2018, p. 30. https://ungc.org.pl/wp-content/uploads/2018/09/Za%C5 %82o%C5 %BCenia-do-ustawy-o-oschronie-sygnalist%C3 %B3w.pdf (16.08.2019).

Cichy, Łukasz. *Whistleblowing w bankach*. Komisja Nadzoru Finansowego, Warszawa, 2017.

Citizens Information. "Protection for whistleblowers," https://www.citizensinformation.ie/en/employment/enforcement_and_redress/protection_for_whistleblowers.html (24.07.2019).

Council of Europe. *Protection of Whistleblowers: Recommendation (CM/Rec(2014)7) Adopted by the Committee of Ministers of the Council of Europe on 30 April 2014 and Explanatory Memorandum*, 2014, https://rm.coe.int/16807096c7 (12.06.2019).

Czerwińska-Engel, Iwona. "3M POLAND." In: *Systemy zgłaszania nieprawidłowości, Założenia do ustawy o ochronie sygnalistów*. Global

Compact Network Poland, Warszawa, 2018, p. 26. https://ungc.org.pl/wp-content/uploads/2018/09/Za%C5 %82o%C5 %BCenia-do-ustawy-o-oschronie-sygnalist%C3 %B3w.pdf (16.08.2019).

Dąbrowski, Robert. "Demaskacja jako narzędzie do walki z korupcją." *Kwartalnik Policyjny* 3/2011, Centrum Szkolenia Policji, Legionowo, pp. 38–43.

Department for Business, Energy & Industrial Strategy. "Blowing the Whistle to a Prescribed Person. List of Prescribed Person and Bodies." 2018. https://www.gov.uk/government/publications/blowing-the-whistle-list-of-prescribed-people-and-bodies--2/whistleblowing-list-of-prescribed-people-and-bodies (13.07.2019).

Department of Public Expenditure and Reform. *Statutory Review of the Protected Disclosures Act 2014*. 2018. https://assets.gov.ie/8765/7e1f2c66e7c04062a25561a848e17943.pdf (25.07.2019).

Derlacz-Wawrowska, Marta. "Whistleblowing a ochrona informacji poufnych pracodawcy." In: *Prawo pracy. Refleksje i poszukiwania. Księga jubileuszowa Profesora Jerzego Wratnego*, ed. Gertruda Uścińska, Instytut Pracy i Spraw Socjalnych, Warszawa, 2013, pp. 390–403.

Dimitriu Raluca. "Romania: First Steps to Whistleblowers' Protection." In: *Whistleblowing: A Comparative Study, Ius Comparatum – Global Studies in Comparative Law 16*, eds. Gregor Thusing, Gerrit Forst, Springer International Publishing, Cham, 2016, pp. 243–262.

Doherty, Michael and Ryan Desmond. "Whistleblowing: National Report for Ireland." In: *Whistleblowing: A Comparative Study, Ius Comparatum – Global Studies in Comparative Law 16*, eds. Gregor Thusing, Gerrit Forst, Springer International Publishing, Cham, 2016, pp. 181–186.

Drozd Andrzej. "Dopuszczalna krytyka pracodawcy (przełożonych) w orzecznictwie Sądu Najwyższego." *Praca i Zabezpieczenie Społeczne* 8.25/2012, Polskie Wydawnictwo Ekonomiczne, Warszawa, pp. 23–26.

Dworkin, Terry M. "US Whistleblowing: a Decade of Progress?" In: *A Global Approach to Public Interest Disclosure. What can we learn from existing whistleblowing legislation and research?*, ed. David B. Lewis, Edward Elgar Publishing Limited, Cheltenham, 2010, pp. 36–55.

Międzynarodowymi Organami Ochrony Praw Człowieka, Warszawa, 2018, pp. 192–197.

Konkel, Mirosław. *Dziurawa ustawa nie obroni sygnalisty*. 2018, https://www.pb.pl/dziurawa-ustawa-nie-obroni-sygnalisty-907980 (14.05.2019).

Kosut, Anna. "Dbałość o dobro zakładu pracy jako źródło obowiązku lojalności pracownika wobec pracodawcy." *Annales UMCS – sectio G (Ius)* 65.2/2018, Wydawnictwo Uniwersytetu Marii Curie-Skłodowskiej, Lublin, pp. 107–115.

Kowal, Monika. "Instytucja świadka anonimowego w świetle kodeksu postępowania karnego." *Prokuratura i Prawo* 5/1999, Prokuratura Krajowa, Warszawa, pp. 113–125.

Kutera, Małgorzata. "Whisteblowing jako narzędzie wykrywania oszustw gospodarczych." *Studia i Prace Kolegium Zarządzania i Finansów* 152/2016, Szkoła Główna Handlowa, Warszawa, pp. 125–144.

Liszcz, Teresa. *Prawo pracy*. Wolters Kluwer Polska, Warszawa, 2019.

Makowski, Grzegorz. *Dyrektywa o ochronie sygnalistów przyjęta przez Parlament Europejski*. 2019. http://www.sygnalista.pl/dyrektywa-o-ochronie-sygnalistow-przyjeta-przez-parlament-europejski/ (28.08.2019).

Makowski, Grzegorz and Marcin Waszak. *Gnębieni, podziwiani i... zasługujący na ochronę. Polacy o sygnalistach. Raport z badania opinii publicznej*. 2018. http://www.batory.org.pl/upload/files/Programy%20operacyjne/Forum%20Idei/Internet_Raport_sygnalisci_12-06.pdf (22.08.2019).

Meijers, Josan. *The Protection of Whistleblowers. Challenges and Opportunities for Local and Regional Government*. Governance Committee, 2019. https://rm.coe.int/the-protection-of-whistleblowers-challenges-and-opportunities-for-loca/16809312bd (06.08.2019).

Mukherjee, Sanghamitra. *Protection of Whistleblowers in United States of America*. LAP LAMBERT Academic Publishing, Saarbrücken, 2013.

National Whistleblower Center. "SEC Whistleblower/Dodd-Frank Act Reward Law," https://www.whistleblowers.org/faq/sec-whistleblower-dodd-frank-act (15.08.2019).

Near, Janet P. and Marcia P. Miceli. “Organizational Dissidence: The Case of Whistle-blowing.” *Journal of Business Ethics* 4/1985, Springer, Berlin, pp. 1–16.

Nowak, Arkadiusz. “Wygaśnięcie stosunku pracy na skutek wykluczenia ze spółdzielni pracy a ochrona członków związków zawodowych. Glosa do wyroku Sądu Najwyższego z dnia 16 czerwca 2005 r., I PK 257/04.” *Gdańskie Studia Prawnicze – Przegląd Orzecznictwa* 4.16/2006, Wydawnictwo Uniwersytetu Gdańskiego, Gdańsk, pp. 165–174.

Nowicki, Marek A. “Guja przeciwko Mołdawii – wyrok ETPC z dnia 12 lutego 2008 r., skarga nr 14277/04.” In: *Europejski Trybunał Praw Człowieka. Wybór orzeczeń 2008*, ed. Marek A. Nowicki, Wolters Kluwer Polska, Warszawa, 2009, pp. 214–218.

Nowicki, Marek A. *Europejski Trybunał Praw Człowieka. Wybór orzeczeń 2011*. Wolters Kluwer Polska, Warszawa, 2012.

OECD. *G20 Anti-Corruption Action Plan: Protection of Whistleblowers: Study on Whistleblower Protection Frameworks, Compendium of Best Practices and Guiding Principles for Legislation*, 2011, https://www.oecd.org/g20/topics/anti-corruption/48972967.pdf (16.07.2019).

OECD. *Phase 3 Report on Implementing the Anti-Bribery Convention in Slovenia*. 2014, www.oecd.org/daf/anti-bribery/SloveniaPhase3ReportEN.pdf (28.08.2019).

OECD. *Committing to Effective Whistleblower Protection*. OECD Publishing, Paris, 2016.

Ombudsman of the Republic of Poland. “The Ombudsman’s letter to the Minister of Family, Labour, and Social Policy, of December 18, 2015, III.7040.104.2015 AF/LN,” http://www.sygnalista.pl/wp-content/uploads/2016/10/List-RPO-MRPiPS-2015.pdf (12.06.2019).

Ombudsman of the Republic of Poland. “Szczegółowa argumentacja Rzecznika Praw Obywatelskich w sprawie zwolnionego dziennikarza Polskiego Radia,” 2016, https://www.rpo.gov.pl/sites/default/files/Polskie%20radio%20-%20zwolniony%20dziennikarz.%20Argumenty%20RPO%20-%202.11.2016.pdf (14.08.2019).

Ombudsman of the Republic of Poland. “Opinion of the Ombudsman on the Draft Law on Transparency in Public Life, of January 22, 2018,” https://www.rpo.gov.pl/pl/content/opinia-rpo-w-sprawie-projektu-ustawy-o-jawnosci-zycia-publicznego (23.10.2018).

Parliamentary Assembly of the Council of Europe. "Recommendation 1916 (2010) Protection of whistle-blowers," 2010, http://assembly.coe.int/nw/xml/XRef/Xref-XML2HTML-EN.asp?fileid=17852&lang=EN (18.08.2019).

Parliamentary Assembly of the Council of Europe. "Resolution 1729 (2010) Protection of whistle-blowers," 2010, http://assembly.coe.int/nw/xml/XRef/Xref-XML2HTML-en.asp?fileid=17851&lang=en, (18.08.2019).

Parliamentary Assembly of the Council of Europe. "Resolution 2060 (2015) Improving the protection of whistle-blowers," 2015, http://assembly.coe.int/nw/xml/XRef/Xref-XML2HTML-en.asp?fileid=21931&lang=en (18.08.2019).

Patterson, Robert. "Compendium of Banking Terms in English and Polish." Trans. Ewa Kieres, Warszawa, 2015, https://phavi.umcs.pl/at/attachments/2015/1211/084950-accounting-pol-eng.pdf (10.08.2019).

Peček, Darja S. "Protection of Persons Reporting Corruption and Other Whistleblowers in the Republic of Slovenia." In: *Whistleblowing: A Comparative Study, Ius Comparatum – Global Studies in Comparative Law 16*, eds. Gregor Thusing, Gerrit Forst, Springer International Publishing, Cham, 2016, pp. 263–278.

Ploszka, Adam. "Ochrona demaskatorów (whistleblowers) w orzecznictwie Europejskiego Trybunału Praw Człowieka." *Europejski Przegląd Sądowy* 4/2014, Wolters Kluwer Polska, Warszawa, pp. 12–18.

Protect. "A guide to PIDA," https://www.whistleblowing.org.uk/a-guide-to-pida/,(13.07.2019).

Protect. "Raising exceptionally serious concerns. 43H of the Public Interest Disclosure Act 1998," https://protect-advice.org.uk/raising-exceptionally-serious-concerns-43h-of-the-public-interest-disclosure-act-1998 (25.06.2019).

PwC Polska. "Kto I jak okrada polskie firmy?" 2018, https://www.pwc.pl/pl/publikacje/2018/badanie-przestepczosci-gospodarczej-2018-raport-pwc.html (12.09.2019).

Rogowski, Wojciech. "Whistleblowing: bohaterstwo, zdrada czy interes?" *Przegląd Corporate Governance* 1/2007, Fundacja Polski Instytut Dyrektorów, pp. 23–41.

Rossi, Ludovica, Jennifer McGuinn, and Fernandes Meena. *Estimating the Economic Benefits of Whistleblower Protection in Public Procurement. Final Report – Study*. 2017, https://publications.europa.eu/en/publication-detail/-/publication/8d5955bd-9378-11e7-b92d-01aa75ed71a1/language-en (14.07.2019).

Save Us Now. "UK Rights and remedies for whistleblowers," 2019, https://www.saveusnow.org.uk/uk-rights-and-remedies-for-whistleblowers/ (12.07.2019).

Skupień, Dagmara. "Whistleblowing in Poland According to Legislation and Case Law." In: *Whistleblowing: A Comparative Study, Ius Comparatum – Global Studies in Comparative Law 16*, eds. Gregor Thusing, Gerrit Forst, Springer International Publishing, Cham, 2016, pp. 221–234.

Speckbacher, Christophe. *Ochrona whistleblowerów w świetle prac GRECO*. 2009. http://www.batory.org.pl/doc/Whistleblowing_mechanisms_REV2_for_Batory_POL.pdf (20.12.2018).

Swedberg, Richard. "Civil Courage: The Case of Knut Wicksell." *Theory and Society*, 28/1999, Springer, Netherlands, pp. 501–528.

Szymczykiewicz, Roland. *Miejsce tzw. sygnalistów w polskim systemie prawnym*. Instytut Wymiaru Sprawiedliwości, Warszawa, 2018.

Świątek-Barylska, Ilona. "Whistleblowing w praktyce. Postawy i zachowania pracowników organizacji gospodarczych." *Prace Naukowe Uniwersytetu Ekonomicznego we Wrocławiu* 249/2012, Wydawnictwo Uniwersytetu Ekonomicznego we Wrocławiu, Wrocław, pp. 403–412.

Świątkowski, Andrzej M. "Article 100." In: *Kodeks pracy. Komentarz*. Wydawnictwo C. H. Beck, Warszawa, 2018, https://sip.legalis.pl/document-view.seam?documentId=mjxw62zogi3damrqgy3denjoobqxalrugi4tinbxguza (11.09.2019).

The Department of Justice. *The False Claims Act: A Primer*. 2011. https://www.justice.gov/sites/default/files/civil/legacy/2011/04/22/C-FRAUDS_FCA_Primer.pdf (14.06.2019).

The Securities and Exchange Commission. "Interpretation of the SEC's Whistleblower Rules under Section 21F of the Securities Exchange Act of 1934," www.sec.gov/rules/interp/2015/34-75592.pdf (17.08.2019).

Transparency International. *Providing an Alternative to Silence: Towards Greater Protection and Support for Whistleblowers in the EU*.

Wolfe, Simon, Mark Worth, and Suelette Dreyfus. *Protecting Whistleblowers in the UK: A New Blueprint*. 2016, https://blueprintforfreespeech.net/wp-content/uploads/2016/05/Report-Protecting-Whistleblowers-In-The-UK.pdf (20.08.2019).

Worth, Mark. *Whistleblowing in Europe. Legal Protections for Whistlelbowers in the EU*. Transparency International, 2013.

Worth, Mark, Suelette Dreyfus, Cannelle Lavite, and Garreth Hanley. *Safe or Sorry: Whistleblower Protection Laws in Europe Deliver Mixed Results*. Blueprint for Free Speech, 2018. https://www.changeofdirection.eu/assets/uploads/BLUEPRINT%20-%20Safe%20or%20Sorry%20-%20Whistleblower%20Protection%20Laws%20in%20Europe%20Deliver%20Mixed%20Results.pdf (23.08.2019).

Wujczyk, Marcin. "Podstawy whistleblowingu w polskim prawie pracy." *Przegląd Sądowy* 6/2014, Wolters Kluwer Polska, Warszawa, pp. 114–122.

Yuhao, Li. "The Case Analysis of the Scandal of Enron." *International Journal of Business and Management* 5.10/2010, Canadian Center of Science and Education, pp. 37–41.

Ziółkowska, Krystyna. "Obowiązek przestrzegania zasad współżycia społecznego w relacji do pracowniczego obowiązku dbałości o dobro zakładu pracy." *Studia Prawnoustrojowe* 28/2015, Wydawnictwo Uniwersytetu Warmińsko-Mazurskiego, Olsztyn, pp. 235–243.

Index of names

Lex et Res Publica
Polish Legal and Political Studies

Edited by
Anna Jaroń

Vol. 1 Anna Jaroń: Socio-Economic Constitutional Rights in Democratisation Processes. An Account of the Constitutional Dialogue Theory. 2012.

Vol. 2 Stanisław Filipowicz: Democracy – The Power of Illusion. 2013.

Vol. 3 Teresa Dukiet-Nagórska (ed.): The Postulates of Restorative Justice and the Continental Model of Criminal Law. As Illustrated by Polish Criminal Law 2014.

Vol. 4 Agnieszka Kupzok: Enforcement of Patents on Geographically Divisible Inventions. An Inquiry into the Standard of Substantive Patent Law Infringement in Cross-Border Constellations. 2015.

Vol. 5 Alicja Jagielska-Burduk / Wojciech Szafrański: Legal Issues in Cultural Heritage Management. A Polish Perspective. 2016.

Vol. 6 Maciej Mataczyński (ed.): The Takeover of Public Companies as a Mode of Exercising EU Treaty Freedoms. 2017.

Vol. 7 Maciej Barczewski (ed.): Value of Information. Intellectual Property, Privacy and Big Data. 2018.

Vol. 8 Pawel Smoleń / Marcin Burzec: Introduction to Polish Tax Law. 2018.

Vol. 9 Łukasz Pohl / Konrad Burdziak: Judicial Interpretation of the 1997 Criminal Code Provisions on Self-Defence. 2019.

Vol. 10 Adam Szot: Judicial Review of Administrative Discretion. The Influence of Court Decisions on Administrative Actions. 2019.

Vol. 11 Michał Peno / Konrad Burdziak (eds.): The Concept of Modern Law. Polish and Central European Tradition. 2019.

Vol. 12 Leszek Leszczyński / Bartosz Liżewski / Adam Szot (eds.): Potential of Precedent in the Statutory Legal Order. 2019.

Vol. 13 Łukasz Bolesta: In Search of a Model for the Legal Protection of a Whistleblower in the Workplace in Poland. A legal and comparative study. 2020.

www.peterlang.com